BERNICE B. LOUGHRAN

CALIFORNIA STATE POLYTECHNIC COLLEGE

ART EXPERIENCES

An Experimental Approach

NEW YORK · BURLINGAME

HARCOURT, BRACE & WORLD

CREDITS

The photographs for Activities 1–49 and 59–76 and the photographs in Part II were taken by the staff photographers of California State Polytechnic College and are used by permission of the college.

ACTIVITY 50 (p. 60). TOP LEFT: Edith Reichman. TOP MIDDLE: Official U.S. Navy photo. TOP RIGHT: Edith Reichman. LOWER LEFT: both photographs, American Museum of Natural History. LOWER RIGHT: Standard Oil Company of New Jersey.

ACTIVITY 51 (p. 61). UPPER LEFT: Edith Reichman. UPPER RIGHT: Nathaniel Nitkin. BOTTOM: Edith Reichman.

ACTIVITY 52 (p. 62). TOP LEFT: Photo Researchers. TOP RIGHT: American Museum of Natural History. MIDDLE LEFT: American Museum of Natural History. BOTTOM LEFT: Carol Bailyn. BOTTOM RIGHT: American Museum of Natural History.

ACTIVITY 53 (p. 63). TOP: NYSPIX–Commerce. BOTTOM: Department of Public Relations, Frankfort, Kentucky.

ACTIVITY 54 (p. 64). TOP: American Museum of Natural History. BOTTOM LEFT: U.S. Fish and Wildlife Service. BOTTOM CENTER AND BOTTOM RIGHT: American Museum of Natural History.

ACTIVITY 55 (p. 65). TOP: Photo Library. BOTTOM LEFT: U.S. Fish and Wildlife Service. BOTTOM RIGHT: Photo Researchers.

ACTIVITY 56 (p. 66). TOP: Standard Oil Company of New Jersey. BOTTOM: Torkel Korling.

ACTIVITY 57 (p. 67). All three photographs by Ylla from Rapho Guillumette.

ACTIVITY 58 (p. 68). TOP: American Museum of Natural History. BOTTOM: Standard Vacuum Oil Co.

FOREWORD

THIS book has been written to guide students with little knowledge of art to experiences in a wide variety of creative, problem-solving experiments with art materials. Participants may be prospective or in-service teachers, or perhaps students from other professions who wish to discover more about art. The emphasis is on an experimental attitude toward materials, not on the finished product. The completed projects are not necessarily works of ART, but should be regarded as evidences of a learning experience. A continuous opportunity for self-evaluation increases the individual's understanding of art structure.

The art experience is essentially subjective. Teaching appreciation without active participation provides students with words to discuss art, but little insight into what it really is. By "solving problems" in the creative use of materials, students will gain insights into art that cannot be achieved by reading about the subject.

Since the emphasis in this book is on the creative experience, it is important that students do the maximum possible number of activities. Such full participation tends to promote fluency, flexibility, and originality in nonmajors in art, perhaps because they have little time to brood over their lack of "talent." An average of about an hour for each project is consistent with these objectives.

A psychological environment free of threats, real or implied, is essential when working with nonmajors in art. For this reason the basis for evaluation of the student work by the instructor should be made clear at the beginning of the course. Grades are generally a source of great concern to the students who have no confidence in their art ability. Worry of this type inhibits creative ability; therefore low grades should be reserved for obviously careless or incomplete work.

Over six hundred students at California State Polytechnic College have completed the course which is built around the first forty-nine activities in this manuscript. The course was planned primarily for future elementary-school teachers, but at least 20 per cent of every section is filled by nonmajors in education. The sense of satisfaction and the enthusiasm for art shown by those completing the course is reinforced as the majority use the adaptation of the activities (Part Two of this book) in their student-teaching in the elementary schools. Their confidence and success in teaching art has inspired many in-service teachers to return to college for art courses.

Although the first forty-nine activities in Part One provide a well-balanced selection of art experiences for the average, basic course, many additional activities are included. This flexibility allows instructors to adapt the material to the needs of their students. It also provides reference material for the future teachers since the sections in Part Two parallel those of Part One.

The correlation between the activities for college students in Part One and those for elementary children in Part Two has been carefully planned to give confidence to teachers in self-contained classrooms of elementary schools. Except in the larger cities, these teachers usually have to plan their own art programs and then teach the subject with little or no help from art specialists. This material may be used as a flexible guide to suggest the long-range plans that every school should make to ensure a child's growth in art.

With ever larger sections in beginning art classes the instructor's contacts with the individual student are necessarily few. For this reason the descriptions of each activity have been made self-explanatory. The aim has been to give enough guidance to lend confidence but not enough to inhibit the individual's creativity or to tell him just what the completed project should look like. References are provided for students desiring more technical details or for those who wish to examine the work of contemporary artists who have solved similar problems.

Society needs a sensitive, flexible attitude toward art in all its forms. It is my hope that this book will guide all who use it to new insights into art and the joy of creating with the hands.

This book could not have been completed without the invaluable assistance of various members of the staff of California State Polytechnic College. Walter Chaffee, Betty Lacey, and Ena Marston of the staff of the Art Department have been most helpful with suggestions and evaluations. I am especially grateful to Boyd Wettlaufer of the photographic section of the audio-visual staff, who collected pictures of student projects over a period of years. The enthusiasm of the hundreds of students who used the material encouraged me to make it available in book form. Dr. Ray Faulkner of Stanford University gave me valuable suggestions on the design section. I should also like to thank Dr. Charles D. Gaitskell, Director of Art, Ontario Department of Education, for his reading and helpful critique of an early draft of the manuscript, and Dr. David Ecker of Ohio State University for his helpful report on a revised version. I deeply appreciate the patience of my family during all the hours I have spent putting the materials together. Mary Ann and Kevin contributed several projects for the photographs in Part Two. Especial thanks go to my mother for what must have seemed an endless typing and retyping of manuscript.

BERNICE B. LOUGHRAN

San Luis Obispo, October 1962

CONTENTS

PART ONE

Creative Activities Using Art Materials

INTRODUCTION

THE FIRST section of Part One is concerned with design. The same principles are fundamental to the activities in the remainder of the book since design can be used to organize the manipulation of art materials into a unified work of art. A good design intensifies the aesthetic reaction of the onlooker. Important as design is, artists seldom agree as to its definition. They even have difficulty in agreeing on a common vocabulary with which to discuss the subject. Here is one explanation of design, with the most frequently used terminology indicated within parentheses: Design is the sensitive organization of visual materials so that the eye delights in following a pattern (RHYTHM or CONTINUITY) until it finds one area more interesting than the rest (EMPHASIS or CENTERS OF INTEREST) and then pauses with satisfaction (BALANCE) at the sense of completeness communicated by the entire creation (UNITY).

An artist works with the plastic elements of line, form (sometimes called mass or shape), color, space, and texture. These might be called the ABC's of art. The design principles noted in the definition above might be compared to the rules of grammar in verbal communication.

A skillful artist manipulates his materials with a sensitivity to the forces within the design he is creating. At times he can violate the rules with impunity. Most people, however, have to learn to perceive and then to use these principles consciously before they can respond directly to the aesthetic impact of a work of art. This is why the judgment of the untrained layman is discounted by those with a cultivated sensitivity to visual communication. Having eyesight does not ensure that you can "see" art.

No formula that you can follow, step by step, will teach you to make good designs. Definitions of *design* are attempts at verbalizing something that cannot be communicated except by direct experience. This is why you are given many opportunities, as you use this book, to manipulate materials and to evaluate the results as design. Perhaps some of your explorations will deserve to be called art. Whether or not you feel each activity is successful, it is valuable because it adds to your ability to respond to future art experiences.

The experimentation and evaluation that you do during these art activities are more important to your understanding of design than the artistic value of your finished product. What is frequently called "talent" in art is not required. If you concentrate on working out each activity, your understanding of the principles involved in artistic creation will grow steadily.

There are artists who will say design is not necessary in a work of art. Their objectives vary. Some of them are concerned with accurately reproducing the appearance of things; others are concerned with using art materials solely to express their inner feelings. Both groups tend to disregard the vital role of design in the great art of the past.

In a sense art is the visual communication of something that the artist feels is significant. A strong design intensifies this communication. Technical competence with art materials frees the professional artist to concentrate on other aspects of his production.

It would be convenient if there were simple rules to use in judging the lasting greatness of a work of art. Thousands of dollars have been invested in pictures which, a few years later, were worth very little. Artists have sometimes died before their work was recognized as significant, probably because the many subtleties woven into a work of art often cannot be easily or readily evaluated, even over the artist's lifetime. However, you can develop a rough measure to use as a screening device. You will wish to revise your criteria as your understanding develops. Expect to change in your taste. Remain flexible. In judging a work of art, consider the following questions and then add some of your own.

1. What is the artist trying to communicate through his work?
2. Are patterns of organization or design used by the artist to hold my attention?
3. Do I feel the artist to be competent in handling his materials?

SECTION ONE

Using Design in Art Expression

THE ACTIVITIES in Section One are organized into five groups, each of which in turn explores one of the fundamental aspects of design. This organization of the activities is as follows:

ACTIVITIES 1 to 6: *Manipulation of Line*
The six experiences in this section have been planned to help you discover that line is exciting to manipulate in many different media and combinations of materials.

ACTIVITIES 7 to 12: *Designs Emphasizing Texture*
These six explorations of textural quality in design should lead to an increased awareness of the tactile qualities of both natural and devised objects.

ACTIVITIES 13 to 17: *Becoming Better Acquainted with Color*
These activities will increase your sensitivity to color differences, helping you to become aware of a greater variety of possible color combinations and the vocabulary needed to communicate descriptions of colors. An essay on color theory precedes the experiences to establish the basic orientations.

ACTIVITIES 18 to 23: *Shaping Form with Paper*
In this group of activities, a familiar material—paper—is manipulated into shapes or masses to provide an easy introduction to the problem of three-dimensional design.

ACTIVITIES 24 to 27: *Symbolizing Space*
These last four experiences give practice with the symbols that our culture recognizes for depicting three-dimensional space on a two-dimensional surface. Again, an essay on linear perspective precedes the experiences to provide technical orientation.

FILMS recommended as an introduction to the five divisions of this design section:

	FILM
Manipulation of Line	*Line and Art*
Designs Emphasizing Texture	*Discovering Texture*
Becoming Better Acquainted with Color	*Discovering Color*
Shaping Form with Paper	*Paper in the Round*
Symbolizing Space	*Discovering Perspective*

In addition, Bates' and Anderson's books on design are invaluable for reference.

LINE DESIGN IN FINGER PAINT

■ *Finger paint dries slowly, allowing time and freedom for the exploration of many types of lines.*

DAMPEN *glazed paper* thoroughly, then spread *finger paint* over the entire surface. On it experiment with making various kinds of lines, using your fingers and whole hand. Remember that lines can curve, zigzag, or turn corners abruptly. Let one kind of line predominate because it is longer, wider, or in some other way different from the others. Fill the background with a variety of less important lines, repeating some types to add to the flowing quality, or continuity, of your design. There will be little or no subject matter; your work will be abstract, or nonobjective.

EVALUATE your design by looking at the paper from across the room. Ask yourself such questions as these: Is there emphasis on one interesting line against a background of lesser, flowing lines? Is there a variety of line types?

ADDITIONAL
RESOURCES: For an exploration of the meaning of line: the film *Line*.
For details on finger painting: Gaitskell, pp. 163–64, and Mattil, pp. 63–65.
For a survey of nonobjective and abstract paintings: Brion *et al.* and Dorival.

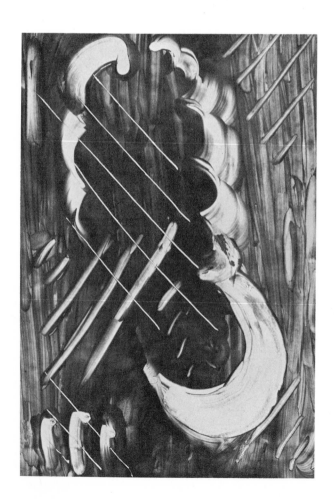

2 FINGERPAINTING—MONOPRINT

■ *A pattern of repeated lines can be used to create a textural background for a dominant line in a monoprint.*

REPEAT some small line movement in *finger paint* on *glazed paper* until it forms a pattern over the entire surface. On a sheet of *newsprint* the same size, arrange a dynamic line design with about a yard of *soft, cotton cord*. Mark the direction of the cord with pencil and remove. Dip the cord into *tempera paint* that contrasts with the color used in the finger painting. Form the design again on the newsprint.

Press the original finger painting firmly onto the string design. For a good print the textured finger painting should be quite moist, and the cord evenly covered with paint. When you separate the sheets, you have the original finger painting with the cord design plus a monoprint which will have a unique texture of its own.

EVALUATE the design by considering whether the line direction created by the cord adds an interesting bit of emphasis to the total design. Which do you prefer texturally, the original finger painting or the print?

_____

_____

ADDITIONAL
RESOURCES: For a further exploration of monoprints: Gaitskell, pp. 241–44, and Mattil, pp. 36–37.
For an appreciation of the role of a dominant line in a design: San Lazzaro, pp. 192 and 226.

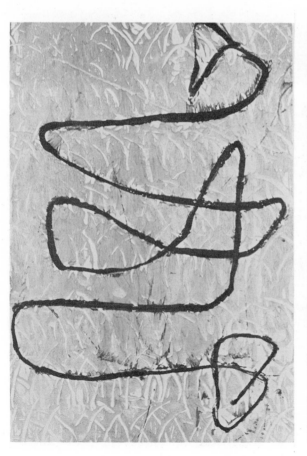

3 DESIGN WITH STRING

■ *Complex experiments with line can be made by arranging and rearranging string.*

MANIPULATE *string* and *cords* of various colors and thicknesses on a sheet of colored *construction paper* until you feel a sense of unity has been achieved. Try many different line directions, making one more important than the others. This emphasis may be gained by choosing intense color or thick cord. Centers of interest can be created by concentrating many small cords until they form an unusual shape.

When the design seems unified, remove one string, apply *rubber cement* to the surface of the paper, and replace the string. Repeat this process until all the strings have been glued to form the original design. A simpler method is to spread an even coat of prepared *liquid starch* over the entire paper, after marking the direction of the principal lines, and then to rearrange the cords while the starch is still wet. The dried starch is quite transparent, and the strings hold well.

EVALUATE the design by deciding whether you have achieved a variety of effects with the string without sacrificing a feeling of unity in the whole design. Is there one principal center of interest?

ADDITIONAL
RESOURCES: For an appreciation of unity achieved principally by lines of different lengths: Kuh, pp. 47, 180, and 181, and San Lazzaro p. 202.

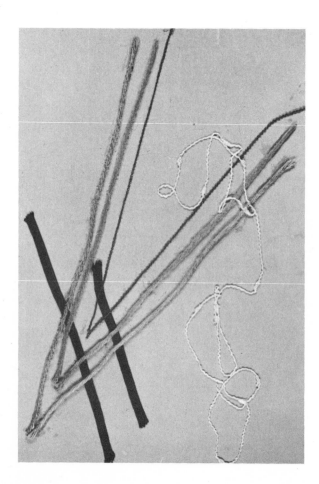

4   MOBILE DESIGN IN SPACE

■ *A mobile changing with the slightest air current creates line designs in space.*

TWIST a piece of firm but flexible *wire* about a yard in length until it makes a flowing line design in space when suspended from a single point along its length. Fasten shapes of *cardboard, metal,* or other *objects* along the wire. Each one should be interesting in itself yet relate to the others in color, form, or texture. One of these objects can form a point of emphasis by its intensity of color, difference in size, or varied shape. Calder has pioneered in this field.

A mobile should move freely from its point of suspension. This can be accomplished by hanging it from an **S** *hook* made of a separate bit of wire, or a *swivel* of the type fishermen use.

EVALUATE the movement of your mobile. Does it create a variety of rhythmic patterns in the air? Is there a point of emphasis? Is it well balanced?

_____

_____

ADDITIONAL
RESOURCES: For appreciation and technical details: Gaitskell, pp. 202–06, Lynch, pp. 7–33 and 88–126, and the film *Making a Mobile.*

7

5 "ADVANCED" DOODLING

■ *Fluency in handling line is developed by deliberate doodling.*

FREELY draw from memory some simple outline form on a sheet of light-colored *drawing paper*. The shape should be large enough to dominate the background. It need not be realistic; an abstract shape can be used. For example, a free form is not a circle, nor an oval, but a flowing curvilinear shape with a few indentations to add interest. Your problem is to fill either the background or the shape itself with an interesting small line design repeated many times so as to give an over-all texture. For further inspiration investigate Paul Klee's free use of line.

Pen or *pencil* can be used in this project. When using pencil, protect the areas already completed from smearing by putting a piece of paper under the hand at work.

EVALUATE your design by discovering whether it gives an effect of texture from a distance. Are you too much aware of the individual little line designs? Is there a clear contrast between the large shape and the background?

ADDITIONAL
RESOURCES: For an appreciation of line used to create texture: San Lazzaro, pp. 19, 39, 50, 53, 67, 71, 80, 87, 93, 104, and 111, Anderson, pp. 53–75, and Macagy and Borten.

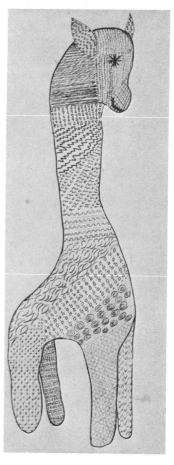

6 DRIED ARRANGEMENT EMPHASIZING LINE

▪ *Natural forms can be used to create line designs.*

COLLECT *dried plants* such as seed pods, small branches, and stiff grasses. Use a piece of *clay* or *styrofoam* as a base. Select one branch or group of stalks to form a dominant line that flows across the arrangement. Place it firmly in the base. Be careful in using verticals; diagonal lines give more continuity, providing a transition from one side to the other. There should be a group of pods or leaves to create a center of interest. Use as much additional small material as you need to lend unity and balance by filling in the background. This three-dimensional arrangement can add interest to a room, particularly in those parts of the country where fresh flowers are expensive during the winter months. The Japanese have shown great ingenuity in their arrangements of natural forms emphasizing line.

EVALUATE your arrangement by considering whether you have achieved an easy flow in your dominant line. Is your eye guided by that line toward the point of emphasis? What setting in a home might be appropriate for your arrangement?

ADDITIONAL
RESOURCES: For useful sources of material: Gannon, pp. 13–31, and Cyphers, Chapter 11.
For help in arranging: Gannon, pp. 40, 47, and 49, Cyphers, Chapter 3, and Benz, pp. 158–59.

7 CRAYON ETCHING

■ *A rich textural effect can be created in a familiar medium.*

COVER a small-sized sheet of *drawing paper* thoroughly with various bright colors, using *wax crayons*. Completely cover this base coat with dark crayon. You will find you can create textured patterns by scratching into the top layer with a bobby pin, a nail, a razor blade, or a similar instrument. Whether you make an abstract design or a realistic scene, remember the need for emphasis. Uncover areas of bright color as well as lines of varying thicknesses. For additional inspiration investigate the use of white lines by contemporary artists such as Mark Tobey and Morris Graves.

The layers of crayon seem to adhere better if the first layer is applied with strokes in one direction and the next with strokes in another direction. You can use *India ink* instead of dark crayon as a covering for your base coat to achieve a slightly different surface texture.

EVALUATE from a distance of about six feet. Does the texture you have created seem rich and varied or weak and uninteresting? Are there areas of bright color for contrast?

ADDITIONAL
RESOURCES: For technical details: Gaitskell, pp. 177–78, and Mattil, pp. 66–67.
For an appreciation of similar effects: Anderson, pp. 56–61, Brion *et al.*, p. 160, Lazzaro, p. 103, and Kuh, p. 179.

8   TEXTURE COLLAGE

■ *Many well-known artists, particularly Pablo Picasso, have created effective designs by arranging materials with an interesting textural quality.*

GATHER *materials* with varying textures—cloth, wood, screening, plastics, yarn, etc. Cut them into diverse shapes, some smaller than others. An interesting free-form shape from one of the larger items in your collection can be mounted on a sheet of contrasting *colored paper* or *cardboard* for an effective background against which the other shapes are pasted. *Yarn, toothpicks, cork, metal foil* and many other materials are useful in developing a center of interest. Try many different relationships of the parts of your collage until you have the unity necessary for a satisfactory design.

    White glue, rubber cement, staples, and *stitching* can all be successfully used to fasten the collage to the background. Glues must be used in very thin coats to avoid discoloring materials. Staples and stitches can be cleverly concealed or made a part of the textural pattern.

EVALUATE by considering whether you have achieved a feeling of variety within unity in your design. Have you avoided giving the impression of clutter, without unity or emphasis? Do the items have a tactile appeal?

ADDITIONAL
RESOURCES: For technical details: Mattil, pp. 119–20.
    For appreciation: Faulkner, Ziegfield, and Hill, p. 423, Kuh, pp. 67 and 68, and Anderson, pp. 150, 157, and 213.

 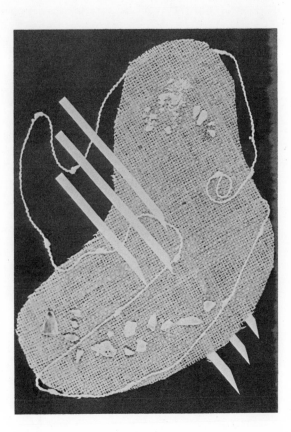

9 HAND SCULPTURE IN WOOD

■ *Experience with the sensual quality of wood has been rewarding to craftsmen through the ages.*

WORK with a hand-sized piece of *soft wood* such as sugar pine or balsa to create a nonrepresentational form. Use a *knife, saw,* or *rasp* to give the wood a distinctive shape that pleases your sense of touch. Keep turning the form so that you are aware of the piece from all angles. Decide whether you need to drill holes into your wood in order to shape interior spaces for emphasis. This can be done with a *hand drill* and enlarged with a rasp.

When you feel that your form is finished, sand it well first with *medium,* then with *fine, sandpaper.* After that polish it with *paste wax* or *shoe polish.* Rub it thoroughly when it is dry. Repeat the polishing, if necessary, to achieve a surface that feels slippery and smooth.

EVALUATE your sculpture by considering whether you have achieved a smooth, flowing quality in your form as you turn it in your hand. Is the finish pleasing to the eye as well as to the touch?

ADDITIONAL
RESOURCES: For technical details: Gaitskell, pp. 214–19 and 328, and Rood, pp. 122–25 and 61.
For appreciation: Sweeney, pp. 34–36, Faulkner, Ziegfield, and Hill, p. 447, Brion *et al.,* p. 261, and Kuh, p. 139.

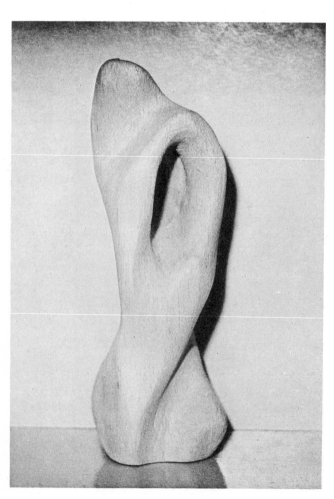

10 DESIGN IN CHALK

■ *Rubbing chalk into paper with the fingers is a tactile experience that provides direct contact with both the material and the working surface.*

EXPERIMENT with soft, colored *chalk* or *pastels* on 12″ × 18″ *drawing paper* to discover the ease with which one color can be drawn over another and then blended in with the fingers. Cover the paper completely with blended color, perhaps subtlely repeating a simple, rhythmic pattern. Against this background draw one or more shapes in a contrasting color of chalk for emphasis. Either naturalistic or abstract forms can be interesting if they are sensitively varied in outline. An area within this shape that allows the background to show through will add further interest. When you have finished, the surface of the paper should be thoroughly covered with rich, powdery chalk.

A slightly rough drawing paper holds the chalk better than smooth paper. Spray the finished design with *fixative* or else protect it with a fold of paper.

EVALUATE the design by viewing it from a distance. Have you taken advantage of the blending and covering qualities of chalk? Do the parts you want to emphasize contrast with the background? Is there a rich, textural quality to the surface?

ADDITIONAL
RESOURCES: For an appreciation of the imaginative use of shapes in contemporary art: Brion *et al.*, pp. 108, 189, 315, and 329, and San Lazzaro, pp. 128, 195, and 221.

11 LITTLE LANDSCAPE IN THREE DIMENSIONS

■ *Making a small-scale landscape reinforces tactile awareness of the world.*

EXPLORE the possibilities of various materials for making a small-scale landscape that will recreate the texture of some corner of the earth's surface. *Velvet, glass, twigs,* and *rocks* are only a few of the materials that can be used. A corner of a garden, an imaginary island, or a large area of unidentified countryside as seen from a plane, are three possibilities. The landscape should appeal to the tactile sense of the onlooker as well as to his eyes. Keep it close to one square foot in area.

As a temporary project your landscape could be simply placed on a *cardboard* base. A permanent production could be firmly fastened to a piece of *wood* or placed within a *box*. *White glue* or *staples* are useful for keeping things in position.

EVALUATE your project by considering whether it has one or more centers of interest. Does one of these points of emphasis seem dominant enough to hold the viewer's attention? Is the texture of the surfaces within the landscape convincing to the sense of touch?

ADDITIONAL
RESOURCES: For technical details: Hammett, pp. 416–17.
For an appreciation of modern landscaping: Faulkner, Ziegfield, and Hill, pp. 34–37.

12 LIGHT ON POLISHED SURFACES

■ *The subtle curves and the shiny surfaces of vases must be perceived before they can be reproduced on paper.*

STUDY actual vases to discover the long streak of concentrated light on those with straight, or almost straight, sides. Observe the curved, almost rectangular highlight of a globular surface. Notice the oval ellipse at the top opening of vases seen below eye level and the deeper curve at the bottom.

Design a vase that is simple in shape but subtly curved. Try to avoid common, compass-made curves. *Crayon* and *chalk* are easier to use in this activity than *paint,* unless you feel that you can control paint easily. Concentrate your heaviest color on one side, then, as you work toward the highlight, lighten the color until the area just around the highlight is barely colored at all. Deepen the color again slightly near the other edge. *Tinted paper* can add a special effect by making the background more interesting.

EVALUATE your work by viewing it from a distance. Is the shape distinctive? Were you able to depict a shiny texture on a dull paper?

_____

_____

ADDITIONAL
RESOURCES: For technical assistance with ellipses: Gaitskell, pp. 170–71.
For help in rendering glass and metal: Kaminski, pp. 56–59.
For an appreciation of beautiful vase shapes: Holme and Frost, pp. 2–3 and 112–21.
For vases with highlights: Hald, pp. 135 and 143.
For painting in water color: Brooks, pp. 58–59.

COLOR
COLOR THEORY

Before you attempt further color experiments you should understand a few facts about color theory as it pertains to pigments. Color may vary as to HUE, INTENSITY, and VALUE. Only a few people are sensitive to the subtle variations in the colors around them, but you can educate your eyes to a new awareness if you are willing to give the time and effort required.

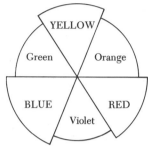

HUE is the name given to the basic pigments as seen on the color wheel. Yellow, red, and blue are classed as primary hues, or hues that cannot be made from a combination of other hues. The secondary colors green, orange, and violet may be mixed by combining the primary colors on either side of them. Mix these in tempera and paint them on your color wheel along with the primary hues.

A VALUE can vary from black, the lowest value, to white, the highest value. Consider, for example, these variations within the color blue. Navy blue is so low it is often mistaken for black. Powder blue, on the other hand, is so high in value that it is almost white. In between the highest and lowest values of any hue are innumerable gradations.

VALUES

Almost black	Very dark	Dark	Medium	Lighter	Very Light	Almost white

To help you understand this theory take a favorite hue in tempera paint and work out a seven-step graduated scale from very low to very high value. Add black to the hue to darken or lower the value and white or water to lighten or raise the value.

INTENSITY is a measure of the amount of the original hue in a color sample. The color as seen on the color wheel is supposed to represent that hue at its highest intensity. When you modify it by adding black, white, or the complement, you lower the intensity or saturation of the original hue. Adding to the color may or may not change its value.

For an illustration of this theory consider blue again. Very little blue pigment is visible in navy blue, so it is low in intensity as well as in value. Perhaps you can imagine another blue that glows with color although its value is very low. This has been called bright navy or deep royal blue. It is medium, rather than low, in intensity. Powder blue, which is very high in value, is low in intensity, but with the addition of more pure pigment it could become more intense and yet remain high in value. It might then be called sky blue, or some similar name.

One of the best ways to lower the intensity of a color without radically changing its value is to add some of its complement. The complement is the hue directly across the circle on the color wheel. To aid your understanding of intensity take a hue from the color wheel and gradually lower its intensity by adding its complement. Try to make the change to a neutral gradually. It becomes a neutral when you cannot identify the original color in the grayed mixture.

INTENSITIES

Highest Intensity	Less Intense	Slightly grayed	Somewhat grayed	Little color	Neutral color

16

Test your knowledge of color terminology by indicating the hue, value, and intensity of the following common colors.*

	BASIC HUE	VALUE	INTENSITY
Navy blue	blue	low	low
Maroon			
Brown			
Pink			

ADDITIONAL RESOURCES: Gaitskell, pp. 168–69, Faulkner, Ziegfield, and Hill, pp. 334–45, and Anderson, pp. 163–69.

There are various ways of classifying color combinations, but these classifications should never be treated as recipes that tell you what colors you should use together. Your sensitivity to colors, innate or learned, is your only assurance that you will combine colors with skill. However, a few commonly used terms are explained here.

A MONOCHROMATIC color scheme is a combination of several values and intensities within one basic hue.

AN ANALOGOUS color scheme is made from various values and intensities derived from several colors next to each other on the color wheel.

A COMPLEMENTARY color scheme is based on various values and intensities of hues opposite each other on the color wheel.

You can create both good and poor color combinations while working within the framework of any of the above schemes. This is one area in which there is no substitute for learning by doing. Working with color and evaluating the results will help you to become more sensitive and skillful in its use. This is the goal of all the experiences with color in this book. Keep in mind the following suggestions:

1. Most people are not fully aware of the infinite possibilities for variation within any one hue. For this reason they use too many different basic hues together.

2. There is a common tendency for people to combine several intense hues in a color combination without realizing that even one can become too dominant. Use hues at full intensity very sparingly.

3. Few people use effectively the less intense, somewhat neutralized variations on a basic hue. Try to include one or more of these in every combination of colors.

For a trial color combination try a little dark, considerable light, then several grays, and a bit of bright. This is not a formula but a jingle to remind you of the full range of value and intensity that you can use. Experiment with this color plan within the framework indicated in the diagram.

COLOR
SCHEME

Dark	Light	Grayed	Grayed	Grayed	Bright

Invent many other color combinations to gain confidence and flexibility in your use of color. Collect outstanding color schemes from many sources. A color notebook or file can be of great value to you.

ADDITIONAL RESOURCES: Faulkner, Ziegfield, and Hill, pp. 346–50 and the colored illustrations in Hald.

*See p. 154 for answers.

13 MAGAZINE MOSAIC

■ *An infinite number of variations can be discovered within each hue.*

TEAR areas of any two contrasting colors from the pages of old *magazines*. Do not try to match colors. A variety within each hue adds interest. Draw a simple shape, representational or abstract, large enough so that it will dominate a sheet of *drawing paper*. *Paste* small pieces of one color at random to cover the background completely. Next use small bits of the contrasting color to develop the central motif. The effect will resemble that of a mosaic because of the many subtle variations within each hue. The problems of color and contrast that you solve in this experience are identical with those of the designer of mosaics.

Mosaics take time. Paper no larger than 12″ × 18″ is recommended as a background for this project unless you have unlimited time to spend on it. Pieces of paper for pasting should be no larger than ½″.

EVALUATE your mosaic by deciding whether you have achieved a clear contrast between your two areas of color. Is the effect of each color intensified by the many variations found in the small pieces?

_____

_____

ADDITIONAL
RESOURCES: For appreciation: the film *Mosaic Experiments*.
For more technical details: Mattil, pp. 122–24, Algiro, and the film *Mosaic Experiments*.

14 NONOBJECTIVE DESIGN USING ONE COLOR

■ *Innumerable variations in value and intensity can be mixed from one basic hue.*

DRAW a free-form shape large enough to dominate 12″ × 18″ *drawing paper.* Superimpose a smaller shape on the first, allowing it to swing out into the background space. Add one or two additional smaller shapes for emphasis. Paint in each of the spaces completely with *tempera paint,* using variations of one hue only. This will require ingenuity in order to keep neighboring areas different in value or intensity. Many artists have accepted this challenge of using only one hue throughout a painting. You might investigate, for example, Picasso's Blue Period.

   It is wise to start with a very small quantity of your chosen hue since you will be adding to it to make all the variations necessary. Do you know that with good-quality tempera you can paint over areas that have dried without having them "bleed through"? This means you can add lines or other detail for greater unity after you have finished your basic design.

EVALUATE your design to determine whether your emphasis has been achieved by strong value contrasts, intensity of color, or other means. Are all the areas painted in recognizable variations of your basic hue?

_____

_____

ADDITIONAL
RESOURCES: For paintings using only one hue: Brion *et al.*, p. 87, and Elgar, pp. 23, 27, and 63.
   For simple divisions of space with various values in nonobjective paintings: Brion, pp. 63, 65, 66, 69, 80, 84, and 272.

19

15 COMPLEXITY OF CONTRASTING COLORS

■ *An exploration of strongly contrasting colors can result in an exciting design.*

CHOOSE a pair of complements, or colors opposite each other on the color wheel. Drop small puddles of *tempera paint* in one of the hues on various areas of your *paper*. Blow vigorously directly over each puddle. Coax the paint into unusual shapes. When the paint is dry, use the other hue in the pair of complements to make flowing lines that give unity to the entire design. The result should be a vivid nonobjective or abstract design.

      The tempera paint that is used for "blowing" should be quite thin for the best results. The paper should not be larger than 12″ × 18″ unless you have a great deal of ambition and lung power.

EVALUATE your design to determine whether the lines that you added to it gave it the unity that it needed. Do some spots seem unrelated to the total design? How can you make them seem part of the whole?

_____

_____

ADDITIONAL
RESOURCES: For an illustration of this "chance" technique: Gaitskell, Plate 8b.

 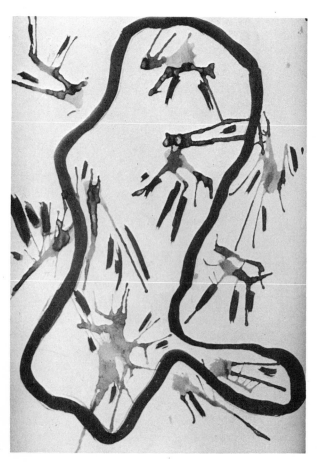

16 ACTION PAINTING

■ *An experience in color using the abstract-expressionistic technique of "action painting" deepens the response to contemporary painting.*

EXPLORE the richness of closely related colors such as green and yellow with all their possibilities for variations in intensity and value. Choose any two or three hues of *tempera paint* that are neighbors on the color wheel. Prepare at least one grayed variation of each hue by adding a few drops of its complement. A half-inch *easel brush* is ideal for this project, but any No. 8 or No. 10 *water-color brush* can be used. Obtain *paper* at least 18″ × 24″ in size. Without prior planning, fill the entire paper with a complex of lines and shapes. The paintings of Jackson Pollock and other action painters listed below will suggest possibilities.

After your picture is dry you can paint over, and "weave" into it, lines of pure, intense color in your chosen hues. Use a light touch to prevent muddying your color.

EVALUATE your design by considering whether the intensity of the pure hues provides sufficient emphasis against the more subtle, grayed values you have used.

ADDITIONAL
RESOURCES: For Jackson Pollock's paintings: Brion *et al.*, pp. 295, 334, and 335.
For information on action painting: Brion, pp. 314–17.

17 A WALL AS A DESIGN IN COLOR

■ *The placement of furniture, windows and other fixtures creates a color design against a wall.*

SKETCH a highly simplified, almost abstract drawing of one wall of an imaginary room on a 10″ × 18″ *paper*. Decide what feature of the room will be emphasized and draw that object in lightly, avoiding the center of the page. Allow about half an inch across the bottom for the rug. Add lamps, chairs, windows, pictures, and other details to give unity to the design that you are creating against the wall. Try to think of the furniture as simple flat shapes. Avoid problems in perspective by drawing things as though you saw only the side nearest you.

Reread the sections on color combinations, and then evolve one for your wall design. If you have not had extensive painting experience, cover the complete wall area with transparent *water color* in your chosen hue. When it is dry you will be able to paint in the furnishings with *tempera paint*. The pencil lines will show through the water color.

EVALUATE the picture by turning it upside down and considering it as an abstract design. Have you created centers of interest without losing the unity of the whole design? Do any areas seem too empty?

ADDITIONAL
RESOURCES: For designing furnishings against a flat wall: Gilles, pp. 53, 94, and 109, and Ball, p. 83. For some varieties of flat furniture: Ball, pp. 70–71.

18 MAD HATS

■ *Manipulating paper to create a fantastic hat tends to release inhibitions to the imaginative use of paper.*

PREPARE 12″ × 18″ *colored construction paper* by cutting 4″ diagonals in from each corner and 4″ lines at right angles to the edge halfway down each of the long sides of the paper. Manipulate and fasten the edges with *staples* or *pins* until the form fits your head. Cylinders and similar shapes can be used as a base, but they are not as flexible. Contrive *ornaments* of fringed, cut, or curled paper. Wire, cord, feathers, netting, and even Christmas ornaments could be used. Some area of the hat should provide a center of interest. This can be done by a concentration of ornament or brilliant color contrast.

EVALUATE your hat by modeling it in front of a mirror. Does it differ from hats you have seen? Does one part of the hat design seem to be more important than the rest?

ADDITIONAL
RESOURCES: For construction details: Becker, pp. 60–64.
For details of fastening paper: Johnson, pp. 92–93.

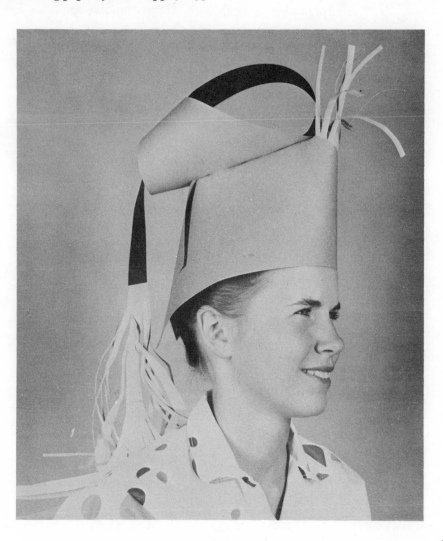

19 CONICAL CREATIONS

■ *The adaptability of the cone shape to many variations is often overlooked or confined to Christmas trees and angels.*

EXPERIMENT with the shaping of various-sized cones from circles of *colored construction paper.* The height of the cone will vary in relation to the size of the triangular piece removed from the circle. Assemble the cones into people, birds, or just plain "creatures." The project need not be made exclusively of cones, although that form should dominate. Contrasting *colored paper, glitter, buttons, raffia,* or *confetti* can be used for accent to add interest.

Small tabs extended from the edges of your various pieces will aid in fastening the parts together. *Staples* have the strength needed to fasten the basic cones together, while *paste* or *rubber cement* can be used in assembling the smaller parts.

EVALUATE your completed form by assessing its originality. Have you shown inventiveness within the limitations of the conical shapes?

_____

_____

ADDITIONAL
RESOURCES: For construction details: Becker, pp. 38–40 and 67–68.
For more ideas using cones: Johnson, pp. 106–07.

20 FREE-STANDING MASKS

▪ *A manipulation of facial features can create original forms related to those of primitive masks.*

ROLL a piece of *12″ × 18″ colored construction paper* lightly over the edge of a table to ease it into a cylindrical shape. Fasten it with *staples* or *rubber cement* to form a mask that stands up. Cut out and add features such as ears and a nose. Explore the possibilities for varying the form by cutting into it for eyes, a mouth, and decorative effects. You may want to roll paper over pencils to make curls or luxuriant eyelashes. Consider a headdress for the finishing touch.

This mask form can be made in any size from 4′ tall for room decorations to 4″ high for finger puppets. *Colored corrugated cardboard* can be an effective base for the oversized masks. Fit the small tubes for the puppets carefully to the size of the fingers that will operate them.

EVALUATE your mask by judging the extent to which you have varied the basic cylinder by adding protruding forms and by cutting into the shape. Have you used contrasting color or some other device for emphasis?

ADDITIONAL
RESOURCES: For construction in paper: Becker, pp. 30–35 and 56–59, Mattil, pp. 49–50, and Johnson, pp. 112–13.
For primitive masks as inspiration, see the illustrations in Riley.

21 CYLINDRICAL CREATURES

■ *Specializing in one kind of form at a time helps to develop ingenuity.*

CONSIDER the possibilities for forming animals out of different-sized cylinders of *colored construction paper*. You could make realistic animals with the distinctive features of the breed, or purely imaginary beasts. A bit of wire may be necessary to make the creatures stand up. Two lengths of *soft wire* can be twisted together as they go through the body cylinder while the four ends each pass through and support a leg. Tabs along the edges help in assembling the animal. Exaggeration in decorative detail such as oversized ears, an unusual tail, and spots, will make the results more interesting.

    This project gives you an opportunity to utilize all the various techniques for manipulating paper that you have experimented with in previous activities. An amusing zoo, with or without cages, could be created.

EVALUATE your beast by considering its uniqueness. Is it capable of standing firmly on its own feet— that is, does it have a character of its own?

_____

_____

ADDITIONAL
RESOURCES: For construction details: Becker, pp. 30–37, 67–68, 74–76, and 84, and Johnson, pp. 112–13 and 163.

22 THREE-DIMENSIONAL POSTERS

■ *Making posters can develop insights into the problems of modern advertising.*

THINK of a short message that you feel would effectively bring the need for some change to the attention of the world (or your immediate group). "Eliminate Litterbugs" and "Speed Kills" are two often-used slogans. Perhaps you can think of a new way to present these or other ideas. Modern lettering is imaginative. Find an example of bold, unusual lettering in a recent publication. Adapt this style for the letters you need in your heading. Sketch them on *colored paper* and cut them out.

Illustrate your message with a simple, relevant three-dimensional object made primarily with *construction paper*. Arrange your lettering and illustration on a background of contrasting colored construction paper or *cardboard*. Plan the spacing so that the words and illustration look as though they belong together without appearing commonplace. Free-form shapes of paper in the background, directional lines of cord or colored paper, or a slight tilt in the message can be useful devices.

EVALUATE the poster by judging its effectiveness from a distance. Is it eye-catching? Does the eye move easily from the wording to the rest of the poster?

_____

_____

ADDITIONAL
RESOURCES: For a general view of modern advertising design: Rand. For help with poster problems: Art Directors' Club of New York, pp. 144–49.

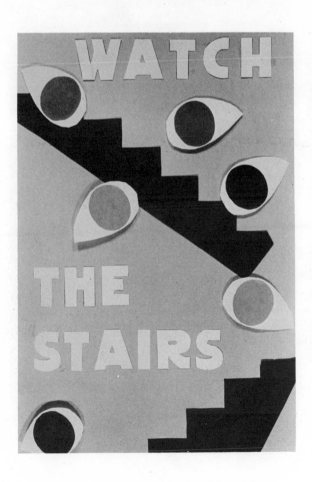

23 DIORAMA

■ *Problems of designing scenery or exhibits can be worked out in making a diorama.*

EXPLORE the possibilities for creating a three-dimensional scene within a small area such as a *shoe box*. A setting for a play, a store window, or an exhibit case are a few of the ideas that can be adapted to the limitations of your material and the small "stage." Include at least two creatures, human or animal, to give life to the production. Colored *construction paper* can be used for the backdrop and to make any needed props. Bits of *wood, wire, sponge,* and *cardboard* can create scenic effects.

You can make miniature people out of *pipe-cleaners*. Center a loop about the size of a dime in one wire for the head. Poke another wire halfway through the loop and twist it two or three times to form the body and the two legs.

EVALUATE the total effect of your diorama from a short distance. Is there a center of interest and action as well as a sense of unity in the scene?

_____

_____

ADDITIONAL
RESOURCES: For more details on dioramas: Gaitskell, pp. 359–60, Mattil, pp. 77–78, Becker, pp. 91–93, and Johnson, pp. 190–91.

LINEAR PERSPECTIVE

Before you attempt further experiments in methods of representing three-dimensional space on a two-dimensional surface there are a few facts about linear perspective that you need to know.

Linear perspective is not used by all cultures to create an illusion of space. Among the many recent painters who have ignored its rules are Picasso, Georges Braque, and Stuart Davis. Some artists feel that its use violates the two-dimensional character of the surface on which the artist works. However, you are handicapped in your expression if you do not understand its principles. It is a necessity in the precise, naturalistic type of drawing.

The technicalities of perspective become logical to you as you use them. Precise methods and diagrams, such as those that follow, are valuable if they increase your understanding of linear perspective. They should not be applied mechanically to all situations. When you know the rules, you can feel free to ignore them.

Draw the boxes shown in the diagram in the positions shown, trying at the same time to understand the principles involved.

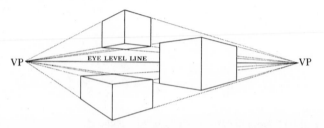

First lightly draw your eye-level line, which is the actual position from which your eyes are viewing the scene. If you sit on the ground, your eye level of course changes. If you climb a hill, it changes drastically.

Next draw three short vertical lines for the corner nearest you of each of the three boxes. One should be above, the second crossing, and the third below the eye-level line. Keep in mind that vertical lines remain vertical in appearance except in the case of extremely tall objects such as skyscrapers. Remembering this will help you to draw objects such as chimneys and windows realistically when the natural appearance of the object is important.

Now you are ready to establish your vanishing points—the points, presumably on the horizon, where all horizontal lines converge.

In this demonstration they might occur where the eye-level line touches the edge of the paper at either side. (In many drawings it is better to have the vanishing points at least six or eight inches off the paper on either side in order to avoid distorted angles.) From the top and bottom of each vertical line on your paper draw a line to each of the two vanishing points.

You now have to decide on the width of the sides of each of your boxes. Lightly draw two vertical lines, one on either side of each corner vertical, between your top and bottom lines, at whatever distance you wish. Experiment with widths so that they are not the same for all three boxes.

From the top of each new vertical line below eye level, and from the bottom of each new vertical above eye level, draw a light line to the vanishing point on the opposite side of the paper. Can you see this last step as a demonstration of the principle that lines actually parallel to each other seem to converge at the same vanishing point?

Do you see the solid form of these three boxes emerging? You cannot see the top and bottom of the middle box because it straddles the eye-level line. Put a box in the same three positions in reference to your eyes for further clarification. On your drawing darken the lines that define the visible lines of each box, considering them as solid forms.

With the principles of linear perspective in mind can you find errors in the drawing of the following house? Correct them.

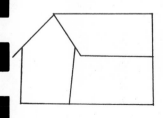

24 PAPER PICTURE

■ *A satisfying illusion of space can be achieved by placing cut or torn pieces of paper on a paper background.*

OVERLAPPING shapes and placing smaller shapes higher on the paper are two of the simplest devices you can use to achieve the illusion of space. Create a picture, perhaps of an outdoor scene, that uses these two devices. Use cut or torn *colored paper* against a *construction-paper* background perhaps 12″ × 18″.

Trees are simple to overlap but the tops have to be different shades of green for the overlaps to show effectively. Fence posts and telegraph poles have to be made smaller as they progress diagonally up across the paper. The limited range of colors available in commercial papers may need to be supplemented from other sources such as old magazines and wallpaper samples. If it is available, try tissue paper in the new range of hues from vivid to gray.

EVALUATE your picture by placing it so that you see it reflected in a mirror. This freshens your perception. Have you achieved a convincing illusion of three-dimensional space on the two-dimensional surface?

ADDITIONAL
RESOURCES: For technical details: Gaitskell, pp. 186–93.

25 SKETCH OF A HOUSE

■ *Applying linear perspective to a drawing of your own will lead to better understanding of the principles.*

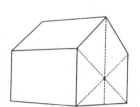

TRY sketching a house with a *pencil* on a 9″ × 12″ sheet of *drawing paper*. Sit where you can see two sides of the house from at least as far away as across the street. Start with the vertical line of the corner as with the boxes. Next put in the base lines of the house where it meets the ground and then the lines of the eaves. The base lines should converge with the lines of the eaves toward some distant vanishing points on your eye level. If the house has a peaked roof, mark a light *x* diagonally between the tops and bottoms of the verticals on that side. An imaginary vertical through the center of the *x* will establish the placement of the peak.

Keep in mind at all times the basic box shape of the house. Put in the big shapes first and then work down to the details. Do not spend more than an hour on the drawing. Try as many sketches as you have time for, letting them get freer and less dependent on eye-level lines and vanishing points.

EVALUATE your drawing by looking at a mirror image of it or exchange drawings with a friend and evaluate each other's. Correct any discrepancy.

_____

ADDITIONAL
RESOURCES: For further help with perspective: Lawson.

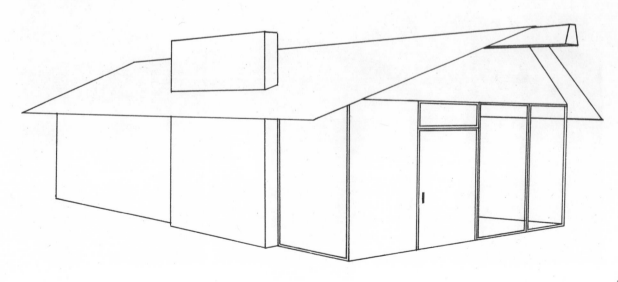

26 WATER-COLOR WASH

■ *While water-color wash is only one of the many water-color techniques, acquiring the control necessary for an even wash lends confidence to other ventures in water color.*

LOAD a large water-color *brush* with sky-colored *water-color paint* and then sweep across the top of a 12″ × 18″ sheet of heavy white *paper*. Quickly coax the color down the paper, reloading the brush with paint when necessary. (Make large quantities of each color so that you don't have to stop to mix more in the middle of a stroke.) After the first few inches dip the brush in water so that the color gradually fades without lines appearing. Turn the paper around and try another graduated wash for the ground color. Note the illusion of distance created by the lighter values. Other details, such as mountains, can be painted in when the background is dry, but your success in water color is quite dependent on your not working over the colors you have already painted.

"Wash" is just one of many ways to handle water color. Others are suggested below.

EVALUATE your washes by considering whether they are even or interrupted by unintentional edges of color. Does your color have a fresh, vibrant quality or does it look worked over and muddy?

_____

_____

ADDITIONAL
RESOURCES: For a variety of techniques: Brooks, both books.
For a slightly different approach to a sky wash: O'Hara, pp. 27–30.

27 WATER-COLOR LANDSCAPE

■ *Handling dark and light to create form in a water color makes it possible to go beyond the flat coloring characteristic of most beginners in the medium.*

SKETCH on heavy, white *paper* an outdoor scene that includes solid objects, such as a house. If regular water-color paper is available, you should certainly use it. Paint in the background with washes of *water color* as you did in the previous experiment. You will discover that by contrasting a dark side of an object against a lighter value on the other side you can achieve an effect of solid form in space. Add several trees, sheds, hills, fences, and other objects whose forms can be defined by the use of dark and light values. Half close your eyes to help you to see these variations in the basic hues of objects. A great deal of the special quality of water color as a medium comes from an exaggeration of these dark-and-light contrasts.

You will find it interesting to experiment with a rather dry brush to add texture to some areas of your picture. Examine original water colors for additional techniques, or, if originals aren't available, see the references below.

EVALUATE your painting by viewing it in a mirror. Is the picture made vivid by the sparkling contrasts of darker values against the white of the paper? Do the various forms seem to be surrounded by space or are they flat against the background?

ADDITIONAL
RESOURCES: For technical help: Brooks, both books.
For one method of handling dark and light values in water color: O'Hara, pp. 38–42.

SECTION TWO

Using Figures in Art Expression

IT MIGHT seem as though people should be easy for you to draw since you have been surrounded by them all your life! However, unless you are naturally perceptive and have had considerable practice, your people probably look as though they had been drawn by a grade-school child. This is natural since that was about the time you got discouraged and stopped trying. How good would you be at writing if you had let a dozen years go by without using that skill?

There is no easy way, no formula, no gimmick that will make you an expert at figure drawing. But the activities in this section do not require unusual competence. Some of them are "fun" projects, to help you to relax and enjoy doing figures. Think of yourself as starting in again where you left off years ago. You may be surprised at how much fun you'll have. You may even improve your skill!

Most of the difficulties common to beginners in drawing people occur because students do not first plan the large forms and long lines, and then go on to the details. They tend to start with some part of the human body and worry over it, erase it, and redraw it until they become discouraged. Consider Thurber and other contemporary artists whose people have personality. Notice that the large shapes and important lines are drawn with firmness. Details are kept to the minimum. Proportion is often disregarded. Try to see your work as a whole, and work boldly.

FILM recommended as an introduction to this area: *Painting Pictures about People.*

34

28 FUN WITH FACES

■ *The infinite variations in human facial features make painting faces a challenging project.*

OBSERVE the basic shapes of people's faces: oval, slightly square, round, etc. Mix several of the possible varieties of flesh color using *tempera paint*. On 12″ × 18″ *newsprint* freely paint head shapes of various types and sizes using the assorted tints you made. When dry, paint on hair and features to create many different expressions and personalities. One point of orientation to keep in mind: the eyes should be placed about halfway between the top and bottom of the head.

Besides the basic white and a dash of red and yellow paint, most flesh color needs several drops of green to tone down the pinkish hue. You may want to include several of the races of mankind. Add a few drops of yellow, a bit of brown, or a little red.

EVALUATE your painting to determine whether you have achieved a variety of expressions, colors, and other characteristics among your faces. Do the eyes seem well placed?

_____

_____

ADDITIONAL
RESOURCES: For the placement of features on a face: Black, pp. 62–63.

29 "CRAZY COSTUME"

■ *Painting a costume promotes a relaxed attitude toward the painting of people.*

EXPERIMENT freely with 18″ × 24″ *paper* and *tempera* paints, until you have an idea for a costume quite unlike any you have ever seen at a party. The features of the face might identify the creature as human, but from that point your imagination should take over. Build a fanciful hat on the top of the head. Next work down, in bold strokes, toward the feet. Be resourceful in mixing hues so that your color scheme adds to the unusual effect.

The use of the large sheet of paper gives most people a feeling of freedom. Large, flat, *easel brushes* also encourage broad effects. Details can be painted on the first coat after it is dry.

EVALUATE your creation by looking at it from a distance. Have you achieved an original effect in the costume you have designed?

_____

_____

30 SOLID FACES

■ *Careful observation is the first step in making a head appear as a solid form on paper.*

USE the side of a short piece of *wax crayon* to make a large face shape on 12″ × 18″ *drawing paper*. Have someone stand facing you with a light hitting his face from one side. Half close your eyes. Note how the form of the face is defined by areas of lower value. These generally occur around the eyes, under the cheek bones, down the side of the nose, and under the chin. Lightly sketch the position of the eyes about halfway between the top and bottom of the head. Now use the side of a dark crayon to indicate where you see values lower than the basic flesh color. Study particularly how the nose is formed, not so much by lines as by darker values. Add hair and other details.

Practice using the side of the crayon until you can produce a gradation from low to high value with a single, controlled stroke. Try using green, orange, and other colors blended into the basic skin color to add a vibrant effect.

EVALUATE the solidity of your face by reflecting the picture in a mirror. Have you succeeded in making the nose look like a projecting form, or is it flat and formless? How many hues have you used to make the color of the skin?

_____

_____

ADDITIONAL
RESOURCES: For technical help in giving form to the face: Black, pp. 70–75.

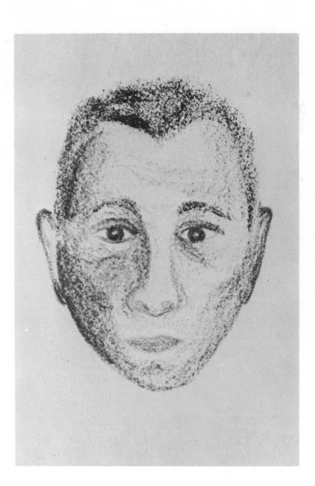

31 FIVE'S A CROWD

■ *In this project the appearance of figures in action is more important than details or proportion.*

EXPERIMENT until you can easily create a human body in action using the side of a short piece of orange *crayon*. These people should have more substance than the usual stick figures. The crayon stroke creates the basic form of the parts of the body in action. Observe carefully the joints that give freedom of movement to the body. Notice that the arm joins the body at the shoulder, and that the elbow bend occurs near the waistline when the arms are at the side.

On a sheet of 12″ × 18″ *drawing paper* create a group of five or more people, drawing them in lightly with the side of an orange crayon. Add appropriate clothes by crayoning over the basic hue with other colors. Consider the places where crowds are found. Sketch in an indication of the background.

Flesh-colored paint can be used in the same way. Since *tempera paint* is opaque, the clothes can be painted over the basic flesh tint when that color is dry.

EVALUATE the work by reflecting it in a mirror. What would you change if you had time to do the project again?

_____

_____

ADDITIONAL
RESOURCES: Black, p. 127, and also the film *Painting Crowds of People*.

32 WORKER

■ *Relating a large, single figure to a background requires a bold, swinging approach with the brush.*

SKETCH a workingman on a scale that will fill the largest *paper* available. Work while standing, if possible. Use a *brush* at least an inch wide and *tempera paint* to place big, bold areas of color on the paper. Without hesitation put in the figure of the worker (full length or just the upper half) and sufficient background to suggest the location where he works. Add details later, when the paint is dry, by painting on top of the first coat with a smaller brush.

If you have time, do several large pictures featuring people. Inexpensive newsprint can give you the freedom to discard unsuccessful starts. Try *chalk* or *charcoal* for flexibility. Decide which medium you prefer.

EVALUATE your work from a distance. Is there a feeling of vitality in your portrayal of the worker? Does the completed picture have a feeling of unity that brings the background and figure together?

_____

_____

ADDITIONAL
RESOURCES: The film *Painting Pictures about People*.

33 MEN FROM PLANET X

■ *Letting the imagination run wild will help to solve the complex problem of painting figures in relation to a landscape.*

CONSIDER what people from another planet might look like. Use a sheet of *paper* at least 18″ × 24″ and preferably larger. *Paint* two or more of these people against an imaginative backdrop of their own environment. Their dwellings, transportation, animals, and plant life would probably differ from ours. Develop a point of emphasis to which other things relate. Work to cover every square inch of paper with paint, but vary the values or hues so that each object will contrast with its background. The greatest contrast should be concentrated in the center of interest. Objects there should be larger, brighter, darker, or lighter than elsewhere.

Have a small quantity of each basic hue close by so that you will be able to change the value and intensity of your colors with ease. A *palette* or *lid* with small depressions is excellent for this.

After completing this picture you might try a similar landscape with people from our own planet. This will seem more difficult because you will be trying to make it look "real." Instead, concentrate on creating a well-designed picture with good emphasis.

EVALUATE your design to determine whether you have achieved the contrast that enables you to see your picture in detail from across the room.

ADDITIONAL
RESOURCES: For unusual concepts of animals and people: Kaminski, pp. 69–75; of other worlds: Rathbun and Hayes, pp. 97, 107, and 109.

34 FACIAL EXPRESSIONS

■ *Careful observation of the human face will reveal close relationships between emotions and changing facial forms.*

OBSERVE people as they change their facial expressions to indicate happiness or sadness. Choose a mood reflected in a person's face to paint with *tempera* on large, 18″ × 24″ *paper*. Start with the basic head shape in flesh color and build on it a feeling of form and expression. An inch-square cellulose *sponge* is useful for defining form with darker values of the skin color. Add neck and shoulders if you wish.

Identify the facial features that change to express the various moods. The mouth, for example, turns up with happiness, down with sadness. Lines appear and disappear around the eyes and mouth. Sometimes artists exaggerate these changes.

Decide whether brown or a combination of brown, green, and other hues should be used to make the lower values that you will need to give your head solidity. Scattering small hints of orange and purple in various areas will give life to the skin tone.

EVALUATE whether you have achieved a feeling of form in your painting of a head without muddying the flesh color. What features most clearly reflect the mood of the subject?

ADDITIONAL
RESOURCES: The film *Painting Pictures about People*.

35 QUICK SKETCHES OF PEOPLE

■ *Several successful experiences in depicting people will give you confidence to sketch from life.*

EXPERIMENT with five- or ten-minute sketches of fellow students on large *newsprint*. Try a variety of media, changing every few sketches to a different one. *Charcoal,* a felt-tip *pen, chalk,* soft lead *pencil,* and *tempera paint* are among the possibilities. Lightly sketch in the large shapes and proportions, then boldly put in the important details. Try to indicate the solid form of the body in at least one of your sketches. Using pressure on one end of the side of your chalk or charcoal can give you a graduated effect with one stroke. This kind of stroke is useful in defining form.

Try a variety of technical approaches. For one drawing keep your eyes on the model, rather than the paper, as your hand sketches in the main directional lines. Another technique, contour drawing, emphasizes the use of a more or less continuous line defining the contours of the model and his features.

EVALUATE your sketches by spreading them out so that you can see them all at one time. Choose the one with the most vitality and character. Which medium did you find the most responsive for this project?

_____

_____

ADDITIONAL
RESOURCES: For the use of a simple directional line: Black, pp. 12–16.
For other approaches: Nicolaides.

SECTION THREE

Using Subjective Experiences in Art Expression

ARTISTS cannot help reflecting their individual reactions in their work unless they are producing mechanical drawings. The degree of importance an artist may attach to self-expression as the justification for his creations varies widely. If he is attempting to paint a particular scene in a somewhat photographic manner, the individuality may be difficult to discern. To some contemporary artists, however, self-expression is sufficient justification for the existence of a painting. Expressionists, abstract expressionists, and nonobjective painters often reflect this concept.

Many psychologists feel this type of painting has a therapeutic value for the artist. Some find it helpful in diagnosing aberrations. A few lay people feel that they can interpret the artist from his work, but this is beyond their competency.

You will probably find free expression in the form of painting an exhilarating experience. Relax as you realize that painting is not a verbal experience. Art is a visual expression. Do not let your conscious mind get in your way! Let free association work for you. Experiment with the most unusual interpretation that occurs to you.

Those who devote their lives to the visual arts usually have a reservoir of images they feel must be expressed or communicated to the rest of the world. Most other people feel handicapped or are inhibited in this respect. The list of suggestions for subjective expression on page 112 will give you ideas to start with. Avoid the obvious interpretation. Try a different idea in each of the experiments in this section. Feel the challenge of self-expression! Enjoy yourself!

FILMS recommended as an introduction to this area: *New Ways of Seeing* and *Mark Tobey: Artist.*
BOOKS: Anderson, pp. 206–15, Kuh, Kepes, and Wight *et al.*

36 DRY-BRUSH TECHNIQUE

■ *Facility in handling paint on an almost dry brush makes unlimited textural effects possible.*

EXPLORE the variety of textures that can be created by painting with very little paint on the brush. Dip a straight-edged, easel-type *brush* into *tempera paint.* Wipe most of it off on the side of the container. With very little pressure apply the brush lightly to the *drawing paper.* The individual bristle marks should be quite visible. Try graduated effects from low to high value with one stroke. This is done by varying the pressure. Interspersing many colors gives very effective results.

Choose a highly personal interpretation of a subject that can make use of the textural effects of the dry brush. The nebulous quality of a dream, or the effect of storm on a landscape are two possibilities. Many of Cézanne's paintings show evidence of form created with the brush stroke.

EVALUATE your picture by viewing it several days after you finish it. Have you created a center of interest by value change or some other method for achieving contrast? Is the brush texture of the painting rich and varied?

ADDITIONAL
RESOURCES: For textural effects similar to those made by using a dry brush and tempera paint: Dorival, pp. 53, 55, and 64.

37 PEN AND INK

■ *Using a familiar tool, such as a pen, to create an unfamiliar effect develops flexibility.*

CREATING simple, even lines with a pen is something you've been doing for years. This project requires that you think of a pen as an instrument for creating a wide range of effects—texture, form, and lines of varied width. Assemble an assortment of *pen points* from the broad, straight type used in lettering to a fine, pointed, flexible nib. Experiment with the lines made by each in turn and then in combination, using *India ink.*

Choose a subjective theme that does not require color but will benefit by the use of a strong dark and light pattern. Do not depend on line alone. Use textured areas and perhaps some that are almost solid and dark in value.

Some people who find prior association inhibiting when working with a pen have used a roughly pointed stick dipped in ink with great success. Several artists have been known to achieve sensitive, casual effects with this method.

EVALUATE your picture by half closing your eyes and determining whether a pattern of dark and light is visible in it. Does the pattern focus attention on the important areas?

_____

_____

ADDITIONAL
RESOURCES: For varied techniques: Hoar, Anderson, Chapter 4, Bates, pp. 30–37, and Museum of Modern Art, pp. 20–21, 34–37, and 40–41.

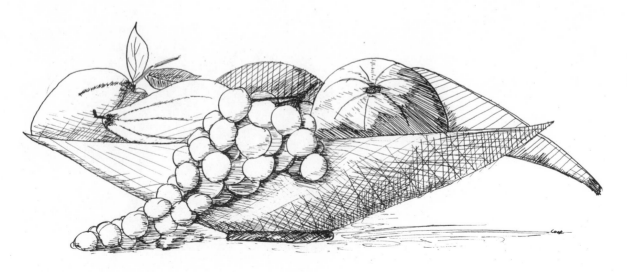

38 CRAYON-RESIST TECHNIQUE

■ *This combination of media has been a challenge to serious artists such as Henry Moore as well as to beginners.*

DISCOVER the unusual textures that can be created by covering areas of *wax crayon* on 12″ × 18″ *paper* with a wash of *water color*. Choose a subject that can be drawn simply in various hues of crayon. A night scene focusing on some unusual happening or a prized possession are two suggestions. Use the color boldly. Press the crayon firmly. Next cover the entire paper with a wash of water color or diluted tempera paint. Choose a hue that will contrast with most of the colors that you used in wax crayon.

Various brands of wax crayon seem to differ in their resistance to water color. Experiment to discover the degree of pressure needed with your crayons to ensure that the wax will show through the paint.

EVALUATE your picture from a distance to determine whether the paint applied to the crayon has obscured your intentions or heightened the contrast. Is there a center of interest?

ADDITIONAL
RESOURCES: For Henry Moore's use of the technique: Sweeney, pp. 56 and 71, and Kuh, p. 55.

39 CRAYON OVERLAYERS

■ *Most people have used wax crayons since kindergarten in the same, flat way, never exploiting the rich result to be had when crayons are used with imagination.*

EXPERIMENT with the effect that you get when you *crayon* one hue over another on 12″ × 18″ white or tinted *drawing paper*. A change in values can be created by lessening or increasing the pressure on the crayon. Artists rarely use one flat color throughout an area. Choose a subject that will allow you to explore the possibilities of overlaying and blending hues throughout the picture. If you can, give a landscape a personal interpretation, based on your own reactions to it. Every part of your scene should be covered with at least two different variations in hue or value.

A tree trunk, for example, might be basically a mixture of yellow, brown, and orange put on in short strokes. Heavy overlays of purple and black on one side would gradually lessen toward the middle to give an effect of form. Texture lines of various dark hues would give the over-all feeling of bark.

Some crayons tend to resist layering. This is particularly true of cheaper crayons that have a greater proportion of wax content. Many students find the semi-pressed crayons more satisfactory because they have less wax in them.

EVALUATE the extent to which you have intermingled hues throughout the picture. Does your handling of color accentuate your center of interest?

_____

_____

ADDITIONAL
RESOURCES: Since wax crayon is seldom used in finished work by professionals, it is necessary to observe color effects in other media—see *Moderns,* pp. 1, 3, 5, 7, and elsewhere, and any other books on contemporary painting.

40 WATER COLOR AND INDIA INK

■ *This technique demands the courage to improvise and to play freely with the media.*

EXPERIMENT with washes of *water color* that broadly indicate the color areas in your picture. Do not worry about colors overlapping or running into each other. Some people like to encourage this happening by dampening the heavy, white *drawing paper* first. When the paint is dry, draw in the details with *pen* and black *India ink*.

It is possible to reverse the process and draw the sketch first with India ink and then paint in the washes of color. However, very few people, except professional artists, can resist the habit of coloring carefully within the lines when they superimpose the color on the pen-and-ink drawing.

You will find that a flexible pen point gives you greater freedom in drawing. Use subject matter of a subjective nature that needs a great deal of small detail in its interpretation. "Lost in the City" is one suggestion.

EVALUATE the freedom with which you have used your pen and water colors. Do your colors "spill over" their bounds in a fresh fashion?

ADDITIONAL
RESOURCES: Raoul Dufy's work in *Moderns*, p. 25, Roger-Marx, and Brooks (1961), pp. 10–11 and throughout.

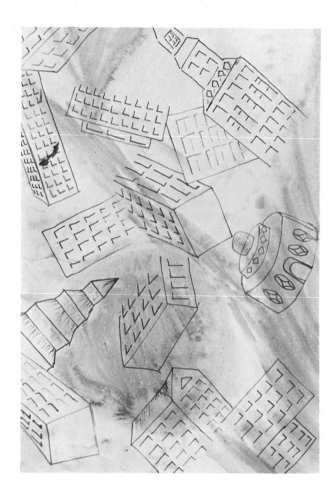

41 CHARCOAL DRAWING

■ *This medium can be used imaginatively instead of being limited to the realistic rendering for which it is noted.*

DISCOVER the range of values that can be obtained with a piece of *charcoal*. A good-quality charcoal will give you a rich, velvety black when rubbed on a piece of slightly rough *drawing paper*. By lessening the pressure and rubbing the surface with a *chamois* or a soft piece of *cloth* afterward, beautiful misty grays can be created. You can pick out the highest values later with a good *eraser*. Choose a personal interpretation of a subject that can be done in grays, white, and black.

Regular charcoal paper is the most satisfactory surface for this medium, although many varieties of drawing paper will work well. A plastic, kneaded eraser is the most efficient in removing charcoal. The completed drawing must be protected from smearing by using *fixative* spray, or placing it carefully in a fold of paper.

EVALUATE your paper with half-closed eyes. Does the pattern of grays and blacks make an effective background for the objects you wish to emphasize in the picture?

ADDITIONAL
RESOURCES: Lithographs and prints that were planned in values of black are valuable to study for their design and interpretive qualities. See also Anderson, p. 42, and the Museum of Modern Art, pp. 16, 43, 60, 62–63, and 82.
For charcoal-like effects: Kuh, pp. 120–21, 126, 151, and 172.

42 WATER CRAYON

■ *The challenge of a new medium requires an exploratory attitude.*

CREATE interesting effects with a rather new medium: *water crayon*. Sticks of these colors can be used dry to produce broad areas of color much as you would use crayon or chalk. It is possible to blend and overlay the various hues to create rich and colorful effects. A wet *brush* will convert all, or any portion, of the picture into a semblance of a water color. The most brilliant effects are obtained by dipping the sticks of color directly into water and then sketching with them while they are still wet. After some experimenting with the medium, choose an introspective idea, perhaps an incident in a dream, that can be expressed in this medium.

A fairly smooth *drawing paper* works well when the water crayons are used wet. A rougher surface is better if they are put on dry.

EVALUATE your picture to determine whether it benefited by the unique properties of this material. Have you used it to imitate the appearance of another medium such as water color? Does it have a unique textural quality that could be created only with water crayon?

ADDITIONAL
RESOURCES: You will seldom find reproductions in this medium. Examine Zaidenberg for highly personalized interpretations of subject matter by artists.

SECTION FOUR

Group Work on Art Projects

THE PRELIMINARY planning of your group should be as freewheeling as a brain storming session. Collect as many ideas as the members of the group can suggest. Each person should feel free to build on the suggestions of others. After a stated length of time the group should determine some method for choosing the idea that will be developed. An informal consensus, or a formal vote, might be used.

Suppose the project is a mural. Once your group has agreed on an idea, you might delegate one person to sketch in lightly with white chalk the space allotment for the principal objects. The others should look on and make constructive suggestions.

After the group approves of the general plan, you can each decide what your special contribution will be. The important thing to remember is that a group project requires interaction. The working atmosphere should be conducive to an easy give and take of ideas. An occasional pause, when the entire group steps back and evaluates the progress, will help to insure the success of your project.

Working with others in this way gives you an insight into the creative processes of other people, which can lead to a deeper appreciation of art work that differs from your own. Working with a group may give you confidence and satisfaction that you have not felt in doing individual projects. If the working atmosphere has been good, with an easy flow of suggestions, the total result is certain to be more ambitious than any one person could accomplish by himself.

43 PAPIER-MÂCHÉ

■ *Cooked papier-mâché pulp is one of the most versatile of modeling materials since it is easily handled and it dries strong and light.*

CONSIDER the possible projects that can be made with papier-mâché as a modeling material while your group tears old *newspapers* into small pieces approximately half an inch in diameter. Fill a large metal cooking *pot*, or other container, with the paper and cover the paper completely with *water*. Drain the water sometime the next day and add fresh water, preferably hot. Bring it to a boil and simmer it for about two hours. Drain off the excess water. When it is cool, add sufficient *wheat flour* or *paste* to make an easily modeled mixture. About a cup to a large panful of pulp should be more than enough.

Almost any small object, from a puppet's head to a relief map, can be shaped with this material. If your group decides to make the cast of characters for a hand-puppet show you can model them right on the finger that will manipulate the head. Some people prefer to make a small tube of heavy *paper* to fit the finger, but this is not necessary.

After four or five days the project will be dry and ready to paint if the humidity is normal and the circulation of air good. Water or oil *paints* can be used for covering, depending on the permanency required.

EVALUATE the projects by considering as a group which have been most successful in utilizing the special qualities of the paper pulp.

ADDITIONAL
RESOURCES: For technical details: Gaitskell, p. 201.
For other varieties of papier-mâché: Mattil, Chapter 7.

44 "TALKING" PUPPET

■ *A puppet whose mouth moves is an interesting variation on the hand-operated type.*

CUT two 6″ × 2″ pieces of firm *cardboard*. Fold each two inches from the end. *Staple* the 4″ end of one piece to a thin 12″ stick of *wood*. Cut a 1″ hole in the middle of the short end of the remaining cardboard. Place it on top of the first piece and staple along with the upper end of a 3″ *rubber band*, firmly onto the stick (see diagram). The rubber band should be near the upper end of the cardboard. Thread the other end of the rubber band through the hole and staple it onto the lower piece of cardboard. The rubber should be taut, but should not pull the lower pieces of cardboard above a right angle to the stick. Fasten a *string* onto the underside of the cardboard directly beneath the rubber at the lower end. Pulling this string makes the "mouth" move.

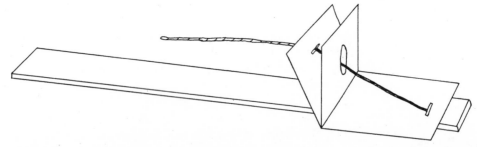

You can build the puppet's face with heavy *paper* forming a cylinder that is fastened with staples to the back of the stick. Follow the directions for cylinder masks given on previous pages. Make certain that you give the "mouth" freedom to move. The type of characters you make should be a group decision so that the culmination can be an improvised play.

EVALUATE your puppets by determining whether the features on your puppets are distinct from a distance.

_____

_____

45 PAINTED MURAL

■ *If this project has been preceded by many experiments with various painting techniques, it will prove a satisfying culmination to the work with tempera paint.*

CONSIDER, with other members of your group, ideas that could be developed in a mural. Plan to use at least five people in action. The general theme "recreation" has inspired many groups. There are, of course, many other themes you can carry out. Use 3′ × 5′ *paper* and any of the *tempera* techniques described in the previous section of the book. If time is limited, applying the paint with a *sponge* is fast and offers limitless possibilities for intermixing colors and textures.

A mural can have several centers of interest, but one is usually emphasized more than the others. Stand far back occasionally to see whether you are getting the contrast you need in both color and value to make the important things stand out.

EVALUATE the mural by considering as a group whether the distribution of hues, values, and subject matter gives the mural an over-all feeling of balance. Are your people large enough to be significant? Is there clear contrast to make certain areas more important?

ADDITIONAL
RESOURCES: The film *Making of a Mural*.

46 CUT-PAPER MURAL

■ *Colored paper, with its strong colors and bold forms, offers a challenge to a group trying to create a mural with a unified design.*

DISCUSS some topic such as "transportation" for a group mural using cut or torn *colored paper.* Talk over the full range of possibilities from outer space to under the sea. For greater variety than is available in the commercial colored papers you can use magazine pages, wallpaper samples or colored tissue paper. Use 3′ × 4′ paper for background.

Step back from your project occasionally to judge whether you are getting the contrast you need. It might be a good idea to assemble the mural with straight *pins* on a wall, so that the group can decide on changes to be made to improve the design before pasting the paper on with *rubber cement.* The featured section, or point of emphasis, should be clearly visible from across the room.

EVALUATE, as a group, whether you have achieved a sense of order and design. How would you rate your mural on originality? Is it ordinary, unusual, or extremely original?

_____

_____

ADDITIONAL
RESOURCES: For some modern murals: Faulkner, Ziegfield, and Hill, pp. 74, 103, and 419.

47 ILLUSTRATED MAP

■ *This exciting exercise in visual communication can be an antidote to a world overdependent on verbal symbols.*

DISCUSS as a group the varied activities that characterize the different sections of your city or your campus, if you are a student. Enlarge a map of the area on a large *paper. Opaque projectors* are useful here since there is little merit in being creative about the basic shapes and proportions of a map. This is one of the few times when tracing or projecting material can be justified.

As a group, think of simple, imaginative illustrations that will communicate to the viewer the outstanding characteristics of each section on your map. This feature could show people in action or could be a well-known landmark. Do not wait until you have planned all your illustrations before you start drawing. Additional inspiration will come as you work. Use *India ink* and *water color,* or another medium if your group prefers, to complete the picture map.

EVALUATE your map by showing it to someone outside your group. Do the illustrations communicate to him without any verbal explanations?

_____

_____

ADDITIONAL
RESOURCES: For some picture maps: Quinn, throughout his Picture Map Geographies, and Werner, pp. 28, 31, and 44.

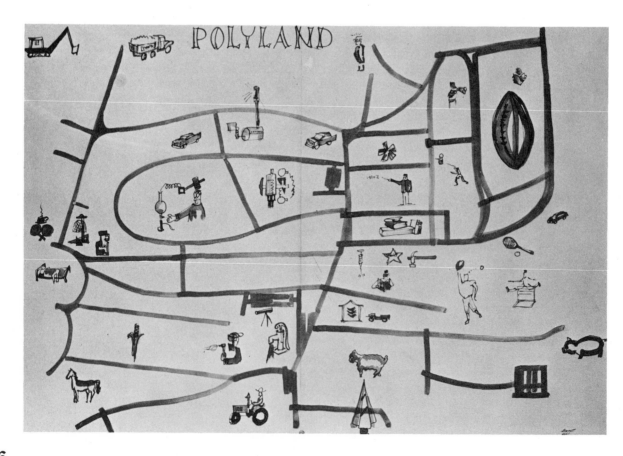

48 HISTORICAL TIME LINE

■ *The portrayal of a sequence of events in time increases your understanding of historical material.*

CONSIDER with your group the many related events in history that could be illustrated in a "time line." There should be at least five happenings that occur over a period of time, yet are in a recognizable sequence. A date should be indicated for each event. Your hobbies, occupational interests, or the subject matter within a particular elementary grade all offer possibilities. Different models of cars or airplanes, from the earliest to the latest, have often been used. Try to find an unusual idea by listing all the subjects members of the group can think of within a three- to five-minute period.

Do any library research ahead of time. Be careful not to have the material before you as you lightly sketch the entire sequence with a *pencil* on *drawing paper* about 12″ × 36″. Depend on written notes, brief sketches, and your sharp perception for as many details as possible. If you reach an impasse and feel you must consult source material, do so away from the area where you are working. Decide as a group on the medium. *Ink* and *water colors* or *crayons* could be used.

Be sure that carelessly printed numbers in the dates do not spoil the total appearance of your project. Make the numbers simple, legible, and yet not too obtrusive.

EVALUATE your time line to determine whether it can be understood from a distance of ten feet. Does it communicate to someone who is not a member of the group?

ADDITIONAL
RESOURCES: For a historical time line: Watson, end papers.

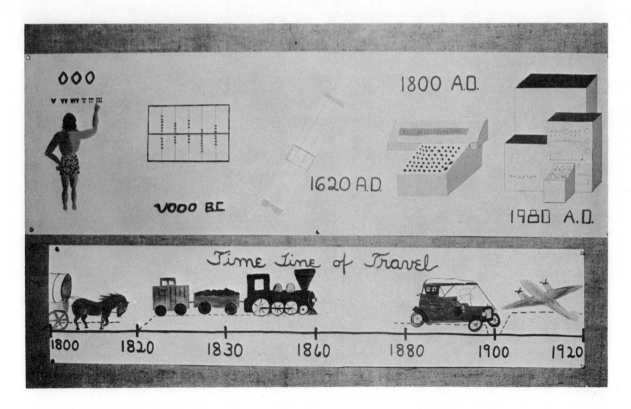

49 BOX BUILDINGS

■ *Problems in three-dimensional architectural design can stir the imagination.*

EXPERIMENT with *boxes* and *cartons* of various sizes to create with them the basic shapes for several buildings. Group interest might determine whether these buildings suggest a farm, a shopping center, a small village, or some similar building unit. Colored *construction paper,* used to make roofs and side walls, can be pasted with *rubber cement* onto the sturdy foundation of the boxes. The amount of detail used will depend on the time that your group has available. Various scrap materials such as *sponge, corrugated cardboard, screening, twigs, sawdust* and *sand* can be useful.

You do not need to fasten the buildings to a permanent base unless you intend to keep them for some time, but, if you decide to, heavy *cardboard, masonite,* or *plywood* all have the firmness required of a good base. *White glue* will bind the cardboard structures to whichever surface you may choose. Landscaping made from the scrap materials listed above will add interest and unity to your project.

EVALUATE the unity in your group of buildings. In what ways do they seem to relate to each other? Is there unity of color, line, form, texture, or space?

ADDITIONAL
RESOURCES: For technical details: Gaitskell, pp. 193–99, or Mattil, pp. 120–21.

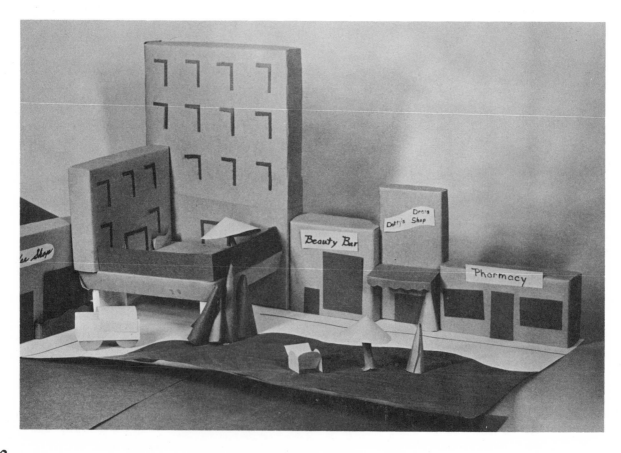

SECTION FIVE

Using Animals in Art Expression

SKILL in drawing animals seems to depend on the individual's perceptivity and his interest in the subject matter. People appear to differ in their ability to see details of an object in relationship to the whole. In a sense, the hand is only the drawing instrument for the observant eye.

For example, an anthropologist gave children of a remote, nomadic Siberian tribe, with no prior schooling or art tradition, the opportunity to draw. The boys, whose lives centered on hunting the reindeer, immediately drew the animal skillfully in good proportions with lifelike motion. For further details on the subject of perceptual readiness, see McFee (1961), p. 334.

There are methods by which you can improve your perception of specific objects. Some of these methods may seem rather silly to a person who intuitively perceives and easily draws objects around him, but they will be most helpful to those who need to improve their perception. If you are interested and want to practice, directed observation, followed by many quick sketches, will help you to draw animals with considerable skill.

The animals in this section were chosen because they are representative of a wide range of other animals or because they are frequently used in art work. There is little point in your drawing every one systematically unless you have an intense interest in doing so, but you might use this section as a reference when you wish to include an animal in your art work. If a particular animal is not listed, you can adapt the questions to another species. If you have the time, it might be a good idea for you to study one of these animals carefully, for if you acquire facility in drawing one, you will have the confidence to attempt others.

Remember that the objective is never to produce a photographic likeness. An artist is always selective. Sharpen your perception of an animal's characteristics, then draw or paint your interpretation.

The habit of seeing first the total form of an object and then the various parts in relation to the whole can be developed by asking yourself questions planned to sharpen your observation. After you have considered the animal, close your eyes and try to recall its general characteristics. Finally, with your eyes open, freely sketch the animal as you see it in your mind. *Do not refer to the animal or to any pictures of it while you are drawing.*

One caution: do not spend time on details and corrections when you first start sketching. Instead, go through the entire process again and again. Each time that you carefully observe the animal and turn away and make another quick sketch, you are enriching the reservoir of information from which you will draw later. Few students can benefit by spending more than an hour at a time studying an animal.

If possible, use the actual animal in your observations. When this is not practical, use a number of good photographs. Avoid using another person's drawings of animals because his perception may have led him to omit or change the very details that you would consider important. Each artist's drawings reflect him as an individual. Past learning and experience prepare each person to see things in a different way. (See McFee, p. 149.)

SUGGESTED REFERENCE: Skeaping.

LEFT: *Drawing of rabbit done before student studied animal.*
RIGHT: *Drawing by the same student twenty minutes later after studying animal.*

50 DOGS

Stop to consider what a dog actually looks like. In what details does a dog differ from a cat? Observe many dogs and then concentrate on one breed for close study.

Does the neck rise at an angle or is it level with the back?
Is the length of the legs greater than the width of the body?
Do the ears stand up or droop down?
Does the nose come to a point or is it squared off?
How many changes of angle are there in the legs?
Does the tail form an angle in relation to the body?

Follow the sketching procedure outlined in the introduction to this section.

EVALUATE your final sketch by reflecting it in a mirror. What special characteristics of the dog have you been most successful in capturing?

51 RABBITS

What comes to your mind immediately when someone says "rabbit." Ears? The unique features of this animal make it easy to identify. Try to avoid devices that simplify drawing rabbits to making a series of circles.

How long are the ears of the rabbit in relation to the length of his body?
Does the oval of the head come to a point in the nose?
Are the ears the same width throughout their length?
Is the back flat or humped?
How many joints do the front and back legs have?
Is the tail a true circle?

Follow the trial sketching procedures outlined earlier.

EVALUATE your final sketch by considering whether you have avoided the insensitive curves that are seen in so many cliché drawings of rabbits.

52 CATS

It is not hard to make an animal that can be identified as a cat. Study cats. Notice the long, subtle lines that flow from the head down through the tail.

What is the actual shape of a cat's head?
From what point do the whiskers originate?
Have you observed the acute angle in the rear legs?
How long is the tail in relation to the length of the body?
Are the ears pointed or round?
Do the ears stand up straight from the head?

Follow the sketching procedure outlined earlier.

EVALUATE your sketch by considering whether you have achieved the long, lithe lines characteristic of a cat.

53 HORSES

Consider how a horse differs from a dog.

Where is the narrowest part of a horse's body?
How acute is the angle of the horse's neck in relation to his back?
Is the neck the same width for its entire length?
Have you noticed how the head is rounded at the cheek and then narrows toward the nose?
What is the shape and position of the ears in relation to the head?
Have you carefully observed the angles formed by the joints in the front and rear legs?

Follow the earlier sketching procedure.

EVALUATE your animal by considering whether it could possibly be mistaken for a dog? Why not?

_____

_____

54 BIRDS

Consider the characteristics that differentiate birds. By including certain features you can easily make a creature that is unmistakably a bird. Specific kinds of birds vary in the line, form, color, and texture of body parts such as beak, wings, crest, and tail.

How does the body of the bird that you are drawing differ from a simple oval shape?
At what angle does the tail join the body?
What is the length of the neck in relation to the width of the body?
What are the characteristics of the beak?
Are the wings small, or do they dominate the body in size?
Have you observed the joints in the legs and the particular shape of the feet?

Sketch a bird as suggested in the introduction to this section.

EVALUATE your bird by considering whether you have given it individualized characteristics rather than simply those of the generic bird.

55 FISH

Webster describes fish as having "limbs . . . developed as fins, and typically a long, somewhat tapering body covered with scales and ending in a broad vertical caudal, or tail, fin." The possible variations in the parts are innumerable, as you will find by looking through any book on tropical fish.

Besides the long, tapering body, what other body shapes are found in the species?
Do the scales create a pattern?
How do the eyes differ among fish?
What is the color range?
How many fins does the average fish have?
In what ways do tails vary?

Make a page full of fish varying in size, form, color, and texture.

EVALUATE your fish by determining whether you've shown imagination in the various characteristics.

_____

_____

56 COWS

Try to recall the typical shape of cows. They are more squarish than most animals.

Is the back of the cow straight or curved?
In proportion to the body is the head large?
Does the head rise high above the level of the back?
Is the head round, square, or triangular?
Are the legs set wider apart or narrower than the width of the body?
Have you noted the position of the horns, ears, and tail?

Follow the sketching procedure indicated earlier.

EVALUATE your sketches by reflecting them in a mirror. Which one has the most unmistakable cow-like characteristics?

_____

_____

57 ELEPHANTS

First consider the shape of the total bulk of the elephant. Next look at various views of the animal.

> Does the level of the head rise above that of the back?
> Is the length of the legs the same as the width of the back or shorter?
> Do the legs have joints?
> What relation do the tusks have to the trunks?
> How would you describe the shape of the ears?
> Would you describe the elephant's tail as wide, short, narrow, or long?

Make sketches as suggested in the introduction to this section.

EVALUATE your elephant by considering whether you have given it subtle variations within the obvious bulky curves.

_____

_____

58 MONKEYS

Monkeys are almost always seen in action. The variety of their poses can enliven your sketches once you have perceived their basic characteristics.

Which is the narrowest and which is the widest portion of the monkey's body?
Could the head be described as round, or as round with a protruding nose?
How do the front legs compare with the body in length?
How many joints do the rear legs have?
Are the ears comparatively large or small?
What shape is the area of skin around the eyes?

Try many sketches as suggested earlier.

EVALUATE the monkeylike characteristics of your sketches. Could your monkeys possibly be mistaken for young children or other animals?

_____

_____

SECTION SIX

Using the Natural Environment in Art Expression

WHY DOES an outdoor painting seem so complex? You may become discouraged when you begin to paint outdoors because you try to do too broad an area, with more detail than is necessary. Look for some small segment of nature that is interesting to you instead of a vast panorama. Cut a frame out of a piece of cardboard and look through it as you survey the countryside.

Once you have narrowed your choice to a certain area, half close your eyes and look at the various lines and forms in it. Keep in mind that man and nature did not arrange the landscape with your painting in mind. Feel free to relocate things. A tree right in the middle of your picture may hide your center of interest and create an awkward division of space.

In a sense, you are arranging the lines, forms, colors, textures, and space that you see before you into a design. Learn to manipulate natural objects when the changes will benefit your picture. Make numerous small sketches of the principal shapes, lines, and colors to determine what sort of a design they form. Turn the sketches upside down and criticize them as designs.

Try a simplified approach to the painting. Once you have made a selection of an area, do several small, preliminary sketches to determine the design. Choose the best arrangement and draw the principal lines and forms lightly on your large paper. Mix all the colors that you will need for the big areas that form the background. At first you may find it easier to have on hand, already mixed, a low value and a high value of each of these hues.

Paint directly and without hesitation. Half close your eyes at intervals so that you can see where the basic hue in an area becomes darker and where lighter in value. Do not work over your colors until they get muddy and indecisive. Fresh color gives a dynamic quality to a painting.

To escape the usual pitfalls of the beginner, remember:

1. Vary your values from dark to light within each hue.
2. Paint the large shapes as you see them, directly and without hesitation.
3. Value the freshness of colors and the feeling that you get when you don't work over your painting, trying to "correct" things.
4. Put in the essential details last of all, and try to keep them to a minimum.

SUGGESTED REFERENCES: Brooks for water color, Leith-Ross for landscape with oil or other opaque paint, and Zweifel for scientific drawing.

SUGGESTED FILMS: Eliot O'Hara Art Series and *New Ways of Seeing*.

59 RAINY DAY

There are various ways you can create a rainy-day atmosphere in a landscape. Consider how the color is affected, subdued in intensity. The edges of objects are often blurred and obscured. Depicting the rain itself requires a "massing" of effect. Certainly each raindrop cannot be painted. People and trees bending to the power of the storm reinforce the idea.

Water color on damp *paper* can express a rainy-day mood, if it is used with freedom and allowed to blend.

Dry *brush* and *tempera paint* might be easier for you to handle than water color in this project. A combination of wet wash and dry brush can be quite effective.

EVALUATE your picture by considering whether the color and technique you have used convey the rainy-day mood of the picture.

_____

_____

60 WINDY DAY

Take a mental inventory of the objects in a landscape that would be influenced by wind. Obviously trees will bend and foliage tends to blow to one side. There are other more subtle ways of indicating that the wind is blowing. Grass and flowers are affected. Clothing wraps itself around people as they lean into the wind. Leaves and paper blow around.

You can use any medium, including *oil paint*, for this kind of picture if you feel you can handle it with confidence and freedom. *Tempera paint* is the simplest medium.

EVALUATE your picture by viewing it in a mirror. Does the technique, as well as the subject matter, seem free and "breezy"?

_____

_____

nearly Blew me away

61 FAVORITE FLOWER

Observe the characteristics of some one flower until you can confidently enlarge it to fill a good-sized *paper*. The design will be better if the center of the flower is not directly in the middle of the page. Direct your attention first to the large shapes, such as the petals, and their relationship to each other. Sketch their distinctive shapes lightly. Observe whether the petals have veins. Is there an indentation or other differentiation of the tip of the petal? Next concentrate on the center. If there is any empty space around the edge of your paper, add parts of leaves or stems.

Chalk can be most effective in this project because it can be blended to produce subtle details and color changes. Since your study is not a scientific one, use your imagination in blending values and intensities of color.

EVALUATE the whole composition to determine whether it gives a rich effect of color of varying intensities and values.

62 DEEP WOODS

Depicting a dense forest or jungle can be an absorbing experience. Think of the individual tree as being partly submerged in the large, textural mass. There is usually much overlapping. You might want to start with the tree trunks in the foreground and a suggestion of branches. Put the foliage in as a large mass, with a feeling of texture but without too much detail. Add shrubs, grass, rocks, and flowers until the group space seems totally occupied.

Sponge used with *tempera* is perhaps the easiest medium that you can use in this project. Try to get a full range of greens from the palest yellow greens to the deepest blue greens.

EVALUATE your large masses of foliage from a distance to decide whether you have achieved a contrast in colors and values between them. Are there brilliant touches of color to add interest to the foreground?

_____

_____

63 WATER

There is no single technique for creating an effect of water in an area of your painting. Collect painting reproductions showing water. Notice the wide range of hues. Examine how the textural pattern of the waves is painted. Find a local body of water. Half close your eyes to discern the pattern of the surface. In drawing a lake or pond in your picture, remember that the distance from near to far shore is flattened by perspective. A round pond would resemble an ellipse on *paper*.

There are probably hundreds of ways of depicting the surface of water. Wave lines will do it, but so will flowing blues and greens together. A collection of water effects for your files will encourage versatility.

EVALUATE your painting by looking at it from a distance. Is there a fresh, watery effect?

_____

_____

74

64 TREES

Become aware of the more obvious shape differences of trees—tall and thin, short and round, and similar variations. Notice the size of the foliage masses in proportion to the trunk. Observe the trunk itself. Does it divide into branches at a low or a high point? Find a nearby tree to draw. Lightly sketch the principal forms and line directions. Half close your eyes. With a *soft pencil*, roughly indicate the dark and light pattern of the foliage without drawing the individual leaves.

Don't forget the dark-to-light values on the trunk. Experiment with various *soft pencils* until you find one that satisfies you. Later try sketching trees in *water color,* emphasizing the shape and the dark and light values in the foliage.

EVALUATE your sketch by considering whether you have been able to represent the form and texture of the foliage without too much leaf detail.

65 SCIENTIFIC DRAWING

There are times when you may need to draw a natural object in fine detail so that another person can identify it. Choose some specimen that you would like to draw very precisely. Look at it from many angles until you have the most meaningful view. Decide whether you are going to make it actual size or perhaps half size. Determining an approximate scale will help you if proportions become troublesome. Begin by lightly sketching the line directions and the shape of the principal parts. Work from the large details to the small ones. If you decided to follow a scale, you can, as a last resort, check the proportions with a *ruler*.

EVALUATE your drawing by reflecting it in a mirror. Are the general proportions as accurate as the small details?

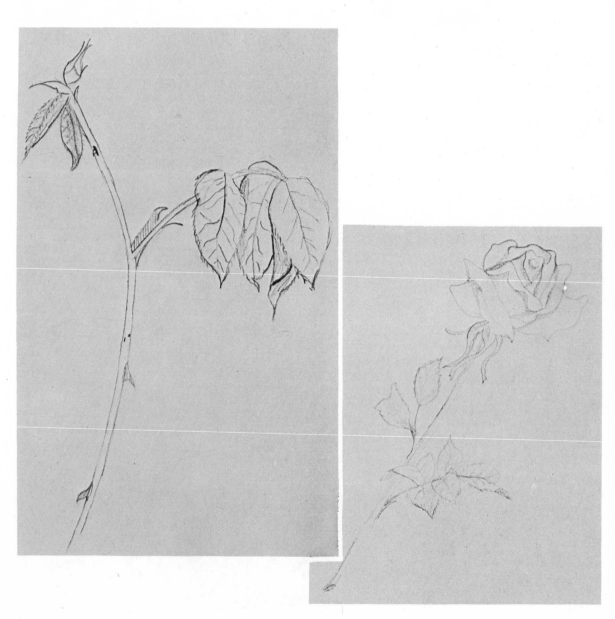

66 CLOUD SHAPES

Clouds appear in innumerable shapes. Spend some time observing them out-of-doors. Note that they are seldom perfectly round. Sketch many cloud forms lightly on your *water-color paper*. Notice how they become smaller as they near the horizon. Brush the area of each cloud with *rubber cement*. Review the water-color wash technique suggested earlier. Let your *brush*, loaded with sky color, skim right over the dry rubber cement. When the *paint* is no longer wet, rub off the rubber cement. Add other features to the landscape to make the foreground interesting. This rubber-cement technique can be used to "preserve" space against the sky for objects you wish to paint in later, such as trees and houses.

EVALUATE the "fresh" quality of the sky color. Are the cloud shapes varied or are they all round? Is the center of interest in the sky or below?

_____

_____

67 MOUNTAINS

Think of the irregular outlines made by mountain peaks against the sky. If there are no mountains nearby, model some in *clay* to get a sense of their form. Try to visualize their three-dimensional bulk, with ridges and gullies to vary the surface. If you are painting, darken one side of the mountains to give a sense of this essential form. Lower values can be used to indicate gullies and other surface variations in texture. Combine mountains with other features in the foreground.

The study of varieties of mountain forms can be an absorbing subject for a vacation sketchbook. Try many media, from *sketching pencil* to *water color*.

EVALUATE your work by considering how far you have advanced from the child-like stereotype of flat, rather pointed mountains. Do your mountains suggest the varieties of rocks, trees, and grasses that cover their surfaces?

_____

_____

SECTION SEVEN

Craft Work as Art Experience

CAN A person be successful in craft work if he has had no previous experience in crafts? Approach your materials in an exploratory way as you did the activities in the other sections of this book. The finished product is not as important as what you learn in making it. Patterns and precise directions might make your first project perfect, but you would be inhibited in attempting further independent work in that craft.

Creatively working through a craft problem, perhaps making a few mistakes, may make your first efforts a bit inferior to the precise product of the how-to-do-it book. The gain comes, however, as you work on the next project. You will become increasingly independent and original as you set higher and higher standards in craftsmanship for yourself. If you are planning to be a teacher, your early mistakes will help you to anticipate points at which your students will need guidance.

Once you have experimented a bit with the material, you will be able to visualize design possibilities. It is not easy to find examples of well-designed articles in the average book on crafts. References following the projects should be helpful.

It is well to be wary of craft designs that are obviously copied from nature. The best craftsmen today are more imaginative. Even conventionalized natural designs are seldom found. Discover the simplicity with which material is treated and the subtle designs that are used in the best of contemporary craft work.

68 STENCIL

For your first experiment in stencil try to avoid natural forms. Cut an assortment of unusual shapes of various sizes from a sheet of *stencil paper* using a sharp *knife* or single-edged *razor blade*. Protect your working surface. If you create a complex of adjacent areas be careful not to detach the central portions. Plan to make a unified design of your assorted parts by their relationship to each other. In painting your material, hold a stiff *brush* vertically, and stroke from the *stencil* onto the *cloth*. Do not use too much paint on the brush. Stippling is also effective. *Textile paint,* or another *paint* that is not too thick, can be used. Mix the hues to get subtle grayed colors. Use bright color only for emphasis.

The discarded *back sheet* from a *mimeograph stencil* makes a satisfactory *stencil paper*.

EVALUATE your stenciled work for the clarity of the edges. Do all parts seem to relate to the whole design?

ADDITIONAL
RESOURCES: Mattil, pp. 30–32.

69 CERAMIC PEOPLE

Consider the idea of making little people from prepared *water-base clay*. Thoroughly knead the clay first until slicing it reveals no tiny airholes. Perhaps you might imagine your little creatures as having wistful, rather than comic or grotesque, personalities. Caricature should stop short of exaggeration. Work toward subtle details of clothing and facial expression. Be careful that everything you add is firmly attached to the main body. Consider where a bit of texture can be worked into the surface of the clay with a piece of *wire* or a *clay tool*.

Keep your people small, probably under six inches tall. Let their arms and legs be very simple so that the main emphasis is on the head.

EVALUATE the originality that you have shown in your small creature. Have you avoided caricature, yet projected the feeling of a real personality?

_____

_____

ADDITIONAL
RESOURCES: Hammett, Chapter 4, and Noma, pp. 30–49.

70 SIMPLE PUPPET

On *wrapping paper,* sketch a 12″ high rag doll with clublike hands and feet. Angle the arms downward. Don't forget the neck. Cut the sketch for a pattern. Form the neck and the head out of one piece to be cut from *cloth,* stitched around the edge, and stuffed. Follow the same procedure with the arms, the legs, and the body. Join the parts with *needle* and *thread.* Joints at the elbows, knees, and waist are created by stitching across. Sew on hair of *yarn* and *paint* on facial features. Attach *black cord* to control *sticks* as shown, balancing the two head strings first. It is easier to balance the strings if two people work together on each puppet while attaching the controls. Keep the leg-control stick free.

EVALUATE the puppet that you have created to determine whether it projects as a character from a distance. Do the arms and legs work freely? Practice the rocking motion that makes the puppet walk.

ADDITIONAL
RESOURCES: Gaitskell, pp. 272–77, and Batchelder, throughout.

71 SEED MOSAIC

Collect *seeds* and *beans* of a variety of hues and values. The local market has a surprising assortment in white, green, red, and yellow. Create a simple design that will permit considerable contrast between areas of subtle color. If you use natural objects in your design, keep them simple against a background of a different value. This is a good project for a non-objective design using nothing but areas of color. After fastening the *seeds* to *cardboard* or *wood* with *white glue*, spray the surface with *lacquer* or frame *under glass*. With very small seeds, spread glue carefully over an area and sprinkle on seeds. Allow the glue to dry, then shake off the excess.

EVALUATE the mosaic for the effect of well-balanced areas of contrasting color. Does the design have unity?

_____

_____

ADDITIONAL
RESOURCES: Argiro, p. 217 and throughout.

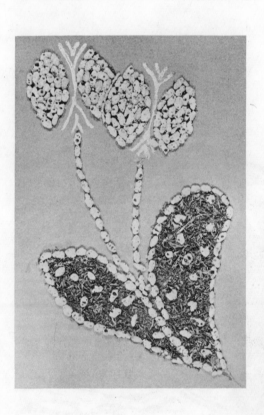

72 LINOLEUM PRINTING

Cut textural effects into a scrap of battleship *linoleum* to get an idea of how *linoleum gouges* work. Sketch ideas for monograms made by overlapping your initials or make a simple symbol for your name or a hobby. Trace your design onto the linoleum. Remember that letters have to be reversed so that they will print correctly. Cut along all of your lines about ⅛" below the surface. Gouge out some areas completely to this depth. Use line texture in at least one section of your design for variety.

Print your design by rolling or daubing *printer's ink* on the linoleum. Press firmly on somewhat absorbant paper such as *newsprint*. Try more complex subject matter for your second linoleum print.

Water-base printer's ink simplifies cleaning up, although the prints may be clearer with oil-base ink.

EVALUATE your print by considering whether you have achieved a feeling of balance in the dark-and-light pattern. Have you worked texture into at least one area?

_____

_____

ADDITIONAL
RESOURCES: Peterdi, pp. 272–75 and illustrations throughout.

73 WEAVING A PURSE

Apply a strip of *adhesive tape* along the long edge of a thick *cardboard*, about 4½″ × 7″. Stick *pins* along the taped edge every ¼″. Tie *carpet warp string* to the first pin. Run it down the front, under, up the back, and around the same pin. Repeat, going down the back and hooking the string around each pin twice—from the front and from the back. Tie the thread to the last pin and the simple loom is warped. With *heavy weft thread*, weave under and over the warp around and around the loom, pushing the wefts close together with a *comb* or *plastic fork*. When the cardboard is completely covered, pull the pins and remove the purse. The weft should lie loosely enough so it will slide off. You can sew a *zipper* in the top.

EVALUATE the result for firm, even texture.

ADDITIONAL
RESOURCES: For simple technical method: Mattil, pp. 107–10.
For further development: Brown or Lewis.

74 SLABWARE DISH

Build up a mound of *clay* or *plasticene* to act as the mold around which a free-form dish can be shaped. An upside-down bowl would be a good description, except that a round shape is rather dull. Cover the mold with a piece of damp *cloth* to prevent the dish being shaped from sticking. Roll to a ¼″ thickness enough wedged (kneaded to exclude air holes) *potter's clay* to cover the mold. Press the clay firmly onto the cloth-covered mold, then trim it flush with the bottom of the mold with a *knife*. Allow it to dry a few hours. When the clay cover has stiffened, carefully remove it and set it upright. By the following day you should be able to gently scrape the surface free of defects and then *sponge* it to remove scraps.

Use whatever facilities you have for glazing and firing after the dish has dried for a week or so. There are good one-fire liquid *glazes* that can be brushed on without a first, or bisque, firing.

EVALUATE the shape of your bowl for interest. Have you avoided the obvious round and oval shapes? How does the finished product compare with the best ceramic dishes you have seen?

_____

_____

ADDITIONAL
RESOURCES: For technical help: Norton, pp. 17–19.

75 SIMPLE SILK-SCREEN STENCIL

Cut a large rectangle in the lid of a *cardboard box* (such as a shoe box), leaving at least an inch-wide margin. *Staple* washed *organdy*, or similar material, so that it covers the opening and fastens to cardboard at the perimeter. Cover this area where the cloth overlaps the cardboard with *masking tape*. Cut a simple stencil, perhaps of a natural form greatly simplified, from a sheet of *newsprint* the size of the lid.

Protect your working surface with *newspaper*. Place a clean sheet of *newsprint, poster paper*, or other thin, absorbent paper the size of the lid, on the table. Put the stencil on top of it and the cloth portion of the lid directly over them both. You are now ready to print.

Lay several spoonfuls of *finger paint* along one inside edge on the masking tape. With pressure, drag the paint across the cloth opening, using the edge of a flat *stick* or a window *squeegee*. Lift your lid and you should find a print. If the print sticks to the cloth and stencil, peel it off carefully. The paint will dry and ruin the stencil if you pause while printing. Investigate other silk screen processes.

EVALUATE the clarity of your print. How could you improve it?

_____

_____

ADDITIONAL
RESOURCES: For technical help: Mattil, pp. 40–43.
For further development: Peterdi, pp. 193–201.

76 WOODEN TOY

Select an assortment of odds and ends of *wood* from a scrap-lumber pile. Assemble them in different ways until their simple forms suggest a play object for children. Saw additional pieces if necessary. Wrap *medium-weight sandpaper* around a block. Sand the pieces, rubbing with the grain of the wood whenever possible, until the surface is smooth. Go over the wood again with *fine sandpaper* until it feels velvety smooth.

If you plan to use several hues of *enamel paint* for a finish, you might find it easier to paint the parts before assembling them. The toy can be put together with *white glue, nails,* or a combination of them both for real strength. Sink the *finishing nails* below the surface with a *nail set.* Before painting, use *wood putty* or sawdust mixed with white glue to fill the holes. If you have already painted the toy, you can mix the sawdust with a drop of enamel, or dab on a bit of matching paint after using wood putty.

EVALUATE the toy as a stimulus to imaginative play. What might a child use it for? Does the surface feel slippery smooth?

_____

_____

ADDITIONAL
RESOURCES: For a simple approach: Mattil, pp. 124–25.
For using tools properly: Gross, Chapter 7.

PART TWO

Art Experiences in the
Elementary School

INTRODUCTION

PART Two has been written for those who will guide the art experiences of children. The activities have been grouped in sections that correspond in subject matter to those in the first part of the book. If you have completed the projects in any one of those sections, you should be competent to begin working with children in that area. You do not have to be an expert to understand the problems involved in a project. Your experimental approach is just as likely to promote the child's growth through art.

The activities within each section of this part are presented on a continuum, with eight levels, which are approximately equivalent to the eight grades of elementary school. Because children and classes in the same grade differ widely in maturity and prior experience in art, the flexibility of a continuum seems preferable to the relative rigidity of a graded course of study for art. The first activities in each section are simple enough for most kindergarteners, but first graders without prior manipulative experience would also find them on their level. Classes differ in so many ways that you will have to decide what level the children you work with are ready for.

There is nothing to be gained by forcing a child beyond his level of readiness in art. Frustration inhibits the child's expression, frequently leading him to copy the work of others or to give up trying. Stimulating projects that he can do will prepare him for success with more complex problems in the future. It may be impossible at times to adjust the activities so that each child in a class is working at his optimum level. Experience will enable you to use the continuum activities above and below the average class level for the benefit of the exceptional children. The gifted usually need less guidance than support and enthusiasm for their creative projects.

You may find it interesting to use these activities while baby-sitting or leading youth groups. They will certainly be a resource during your student teaching and later in your first position. Use them flexibly. Make notes in the margins. Refer to the evaluations you made when you did similar projects. The good teacher of creative art takes time to plan carefully so that the children are stimulated to express their own unique interpretations of the problem. A rough measure of your success might be the degree of individuality shown by each child in his art work done under your guidance.

FILMS recommended as an introduction to Part Two: *The Adventures of the Asterisk* and *The Purple Turtle.*

SECTION ONE

Using Design in Elementary-School Art

OBJECTIVES

To create awareness of the ABC's of line, form, color, space, and texture as well as to increase skill in manipulating these plastic elements.

To create sensitivity to the design "grammar" of emphasis, continuity, and balance as well as to increase skill in discerning these design principles in art products.

To enable the students to create original designs with increasing fluency, flexibility, and originality.

Background information on design and the terms used in discussing principles of design will be found in the Introduction to Part One. The projects are also closely related. The teacher should remember that some children will not be ready to assimilate new concepts even when they perceive them. *Never criticize a child for not utilizing in his drawing the concept the class has studied*. He probably is not yet ready for it.

Building sensitivity to design is a long, slow process. It must be given constant practice over a period of years in every art activity, not just those devoted to design. If design is not relevant, then there is a question as to whether the activity *is* art. With the young child, making the important thing in the picture big or bright creates emphasis. Talking about "filling the paper" uses the child's intuitive feeling for rhythmic repetition and balance.

By the middle elementary grades teaching unity as "Filling the paper with a variety of things that look as though they belong together" seems to communicate meaning. Developing a conscious knowledge, through discussion, of the various ways that emphasis is created is effective. If a child has not been exposed continuously to design criteria before adolescence, his sensitivity will probably have to be developed through conscious, verbal analysis using the design principles as defined in the beginning of this book. With time and constant practice his response may become intuitive.

EXPERIENCES WITH LINE

Lines in Finger Paint

LEVEL I

See
ACTIVITY 1

SUGGESTED MATERIALS: Finger paint, glazed paper about 16" × 20", and water pans.

Discuss different kinds of lines. Suggest that the children look for lines in their surroundings and draw them in the air, and that they notice differences in width, direction, and length. Have them use hand or finger paint to fill their paper with many different kinds of line.

Line Design with Paint

LEVEL 2

See
ACTIVITY 5

SUGGESTED MATERIALS: Black tempera paint, brushes, water pans, possibly wax crayons, and 18″ × 24″ paper.

Discuss different kinds of lines, as above. Suggest that each child choose one kind of line to emphasize, using brush and black paint to place it so that it dominates the paper. He may wish to fill the remaining space with varieties of lines that are less important because they are thinner or shorter. Later, when the designs are dry, the children may enjoy making them gay with colored crayons.

Line Design with Crayons

LEVEL 3

See
ACTIVITY 5

SUGGESTED MATERIALS: Wax crayons, 12″ × 18″ drawing paper, water colors, brushes, and water pans.

Have the children take turns painting varieties of lines on the chalkboard, using clear water. In drawing on paper, suggest that each child choose one kind of line to emphasize, using crayon to draw it large and at least ½″ wide. He then uses other types of line to fill the paper, but every new line should begin and end at another line, or at an edge of the paper. For added interest the whole paper can be brushed over with water color of a contrasting color.

Designs with Colored String

LEVEL 4

See
ACTIVITY 3

SUGGESTED MATERIALS: Strings of assorted colors and widths, 12″ × 18″ colored construction paper, liquid starch or paste, and brushes.

Examine the assorted strings with the children, directing their attention to the variations in color and thickness. Have them choose a handful to manipulate on their paper. Encourage them to choose a bright, thick string for the dominant line and less conspicuous cords for smaller background designs. After they have planned their design, they can paste the string to the paper. Ordinary paste will do, but liquid starch, spread generously either under the string or over the entire paper, seems to produce neater results, since it is transparent when it dries.

Monoprint with Finger Paint

LEVEL 5

See
ACTIVITY 2

SUGGESTED MATERIALS: Finger paint, glazed paper about 16″ × 20″, plain, soft newsprint the same size, ¼″ cord, and tempera paint.

Encourage the children to make up some small design that they can repeat over and over in the finger paint until they have covered the entire paper. Have them arrange not more than a yard of the cord on the newsprint so that it makes a design. Complete as in Activity 2.

Doodle Design

LEVEL 6

See
ACTIVITY 5

SUGGESTED MATERIALS: 9″ × 12″ drawing paper, pencils, felt-tip or other pens, and ink.

Discuss lines created by the edges of forms—contour lines. Have each child draw the contour line of some common but interesting form so that it touches all four edges of the drawing paper. After a review of the kinds of lines, have them fill the inner or outer space created by the contour line with a complex of tiny line designs, or "doodles." Caution the children that a design differs from a scribble. This activity is enjoyable as a group project done on large paper with a brush and tempera paint.

Dried Arrangement Emphasizing Line

LEVEL 7

See
ACTIVITY 6

SUGGESTED MATERIALS: Dried weeds, branches, and other natural material, and clay or styrofoam for a base.

Show the class pictures of Japanese and other contemporary arrangements of natural materials that emphasize a dominant line direction. Encourage the students to use terms such as *balance, continuity,* and *emphasis* in analyzing their own work and that of others. The purpose of this project should be to use branches to create an interesting line for continuity, with the other material providing emphasis and balance. The base material permits re-arrangement until a satisfying effect has been created.

Wire Sculpture or Mobiles

LEVEL 8

See
ACTIVITY 4

SUGGESTED MATERIALS: Wire coat hangers or similar gauge wire, wire-cutters, light cardboard, tissue paper, and glue.

Have the class view photographs of wire sculpture or show the film *Making a Mobile*. Discuss the continuity derived from the wire and repetition of suspended objects. Note whether emphasis is obtained from the use of bright color, large size, or distinctive shape. Consider the swivel devices that will allow a mobile to move. Try covering flat wire shapes with glue, then lay a sheet of colored tissue paper on top. Trim the paper when the glue is dry. Cardboard can also be manipulated into interesting shapes.

EXPERIENCES WITH TEXTURE

Rough-Smooth Chart

LEVEL 1

See
ACTIVITIES
8 *and* 9

SUGGESTED MATERIALS: About a yard of burlap, tag board to fit a chart rack, and assorted rough and smooth objects.

Bring a few rough and smooth objects to class for the children to handle. (They would enjoy the hand sculpture from Activity 9.) Suggest that they collect rough and smooth objects, too, perhaps on a class walk. Prepare the background of the chart by cutting a large free form from the burlap and pasting it on the tag board. Have a committee help to select rough objects to be fastened to the smooth tag, and smooth objects for the burlap. Some mature children may want to make their own small-sized charts.

Group Collage

LEVEL 2

See
ACTIVITY 8

SUGGESTED MATERIALS: About a yard of soft flannel, tag board to fit a chart rack, and assorted soft and hard objects.

Allow the children to handle an assortment of soft and hard objects. Arrange them, with the children's help, in order from very soft to very hard. Cut a large free-form shape from the flannel and paste it to tag board. Encourage the children to bring to class small hard objects and small soft objects. Fasten them to the chart so they can be removed easily. When the chart has become completely cluttered with objects, teach the class how this chaos can be turned into a design. Remove everything. Help the children choose one object for emphasis and discover how a "path" of similar objects can create continuity. Use only enough material to balance the design comfortably.

Chalk on Rough Paper

LEVEL 3

See
ACTIVITY 10

SUGGESTED MATERIALS: Sandpaper sheets or rough paper 9″ × 12″, colored chalk (perhaps soaked in concentrated sugar solution for an hour), and disposable paper tissue.

Direct the children's attention to the blending quality of chalk. Let them take turns experimenting with blending one color into another on a large sheet of paper fastened to a bulletin board. Discuss the colorful objects or designs they can make on their individual sheets. Protect their desks with newspaper. Give them tissues to clean their fingers. Make them aware of the role of their fingertips as they work.

Crayon Etchings

LEVEL 4

See
ACTIVITY 7

SUGGESTED MATERIALS: Drawing paper 9″ × 12″, wax crayons, and small metal objects for scraping (bobby pins, nails, dull knives, etc.).

Prepare a small sample strip to use for a brief demonstration of how scraping the top dark layer of crayon away allows the bright color underneath to show. Show some finished examples, if any are available, then put all the samples out of sight of the students before they begin their work. Explain to the class the necessity for completely covering the paper with bright-colored crayon before putting on the second layer of dark crayon. Encourage them to scratch away with various objects to uncover large areas of bright color and to create textural patterns, as well as line designs.

Texture Maps

LEVEL 5

See
ACTIVITY 11

SUGGESTED MATERIALS: Cardboard or wood for a base, an assortment of glass, velvet, rocks, sand, etc., and epoxy glues.

Motivate the class to make a map showing the texture of the area they have been studying in social science. The map can be a group or individual project, depending on the time and the facilities. Lead them to see how grassy areas can be soft flannel or velvet, while mountains can be built up from real rocks. Have them decide whether it is to be an "airplane view," or a small section larger in scale. Encourage imagination in the gathering of materials. If the project is to be a special, permanent one, the parts can be put together with new Epoxy glues. A temporary, easily dismantled map can be of equal educational value.

Hand Sculpture in Wood

LEVEL 6

See
ACTIVITY 9

SUGGESTED MATERIALS: Pieces of soft wood about 2″ × 2″ × 6″, coping saws, hand drills, a vise, a rasp, assorted sandpaper, and paste wax.

Show the class some wood that is highly polished, letting them feel its slippery surface. Explore local resources to obtain sufficient rough wood for the group. Demonstrate safety procedures with saw and drill. Encourage the students to saw off corners and drill holes to create free-form shapes. A wood rasp is useful to remove rough edges. Sandpapering—first with rough sandpaper, next with medium, and then with fine—smoothes the wood. Last of all, paste wax or shoe polish is rubbed on and the wood is polished until it is satin-smooth.

Collages

LEVEL 7

See
ACTIVITY 8

SUGGESTED MATERIALS: Colored construction paper 12″ × 18″, scraps of cloth, screening, and other odds and ends, paste, and straight pins.

Ask students to bring a variety of textural material to class. Explain collage as a design organized with these materials. Review principles of design if necessary. Encourage students to achieve a variety in sizes, shapes, and colors without losing the over-all sense of unity. Pinning the pieces to the construction paper before pasting permits readjustment to improve the design. (Talented students might enjoy trying to reproduce collage with tempera paint on paper.)

Shiny Vases

LEVEL 8

See
ACTIVITY 12

SUGGESTED MATERIALS: Drawing paper 12″ × 18″ and chalk, wax crayons, or paint.

Have the students examine polished surfaces and analyze the visual clues that communicate shininess. Show them paintings with these effects. Guide them to observe the highlight and the gradations of color around it. Ask them to sketch a beautiful imaginary vase and to make it look shiny using any medium they choose. (Talented students may later draw an actual vase with flowers and then paint it, but this activity might prove too frustrating to some to be used as a class project.)

EXPERIENCES WITH COLOR

Perceiving Color

LEVEL 1

See
ACTIVITY 13

SUGGESTED MATERIALS: Old magazines, scissors, and six shoe boxes, labeled for each basic color.

Collect a pile of colorful old magazines. Label six shoe boxes each with the name of one of the primary, or basic, colors. Introduce the concept of all the variations within each hue by using examples in the surroundings. Have the children discover additional variations. Explain that they are to find these colors in the magazines, cut them out, and sort them into piles according to hue. Each pile then goes into the correct shoe box. This experience could culminate in an individual, or group, collage, although its value rests largely in the training of the eye to perceive color variations.

Group Collage

LEVEL 2

See
ACTIVITY 13

SUGGESTED MATERIALS: Old magazines, scissors, paste, a 24″ × 36″ sheet of paper, and boxes labeled for each of the six basic colors.

Have the children cut and sort colors from the old magazines during their spare time, beginning a week or so ahead. Fasten the large paper to the bulletin board after the boxes are well filled with color scraps. Discuss with the class what big object they could put on the paper. Their suggestions may be inspired by the time of the year or the nearest holiday. Ask some eager child to draw it as big as he can. Help the class to plan the colors and to decide how many may work at the pasting at one time.

Individual Paper Mosaics

LEVEL 3

SUGGESTED MATERIALS: Old magazines, scissors, paste, and colored construction paper 9″ × 12″.

See
ACTIVITY 13

Discuss favorite colors with the children. Ask each child to choose one hue and then cut out variations of that color from old magazines. This can be done ahead of time. Later explain what is meant by contrasting colors. Have each child choose a sheet of colored paper that contrasts with his chosen color. Encourage each to draw an object, or a designed shape, on the colored paper and then fill it in with small pasted bits of his favorite color scraps.

Free-Color Designs

LEVEL 4

SUGGESTED MATERIALS: Boxes of semimoist water colors, brushes, water pans, and 12″ × 18″ paper.

Demonstrate how the basic colors can be varied by the addition of other hues. Explain where the mixing should be done and how the box itself can be kept clean. Review with the children their prior experiences in design and color, recalling "contrast" and "emphasis." Let them improvise freely with just an occasional caution about "muddying" the color. Within the time that is available give fresh sheets of paper to the pupils who complete designs.

One-Color Designs

LEVEL 5

SUGGESTED MATERIALS: Tempera paint, mixing pans, brushes, water pans, and 12″ × 18″ paper.

See
ACTIVITIES
13–17

Review with the class their experiences in perceiving variations within one basic color. Let them each have a small portion of one basic color plus black and white. Suggest that the basic color be used to paint a line design that will divide the paper into areas that make an interesting design. Remind them that a good design has a center of interest for emphasis. Give any necessary precautions for mixing variations of the basic hue to paint in the areas.

Contrasting Colors

LEVEL 6

SUGGESTED MATERIALS: Tempera paint, brushes, water pans, and 12″ × 18″ paper.

See
ACTIVITY 15

Use a color chart to discuss with the class complements as strongly contrasting hues. Have them examine their surroundings for further examples. Distribute thin tempera paint so that each child has a pair of complements available nearby. Demonstrate how blowing directly over a small puddle of paint will make spidery shapes for emphasis on their papers. Guide them to discover how lines of the contrasting color can lead the eye around the paper and give unity and balance to the design.

Imaginary Flowers

LEVEL 7

See
ACTIVITY 61

SUGGESTED MATERIALS: Tempera paint, mixing pans, water pans, brushes, and 12″ × 18″ paper (black might be used).

Demonstrate for the class how hues can be grayed or dulled by adding their complements. Distribute paint so that each student has a pair of complements available. Discuss the infinite variety of imaginary flower shapes that can be created. Encourage students to paint petal shapes directly on the paper with grayed hues. After the grayed flowers are dry, the pure hues can be used to paint line designs onto the flowers to make them gay and add needed emphasis.

Wall Designs

LEVEL 8

See
ACTIVITY 17

SUGGESTED MATERIALS: Tempera paint, mixing pans, water pans, brushes, and 9″ × 18″ paper in pale or neutral hues.

Help the students to perceive various pieces of furniture as making distinctive, flat shapes against a wall. Indicate that they can consider their paper as a side wall of an imaginary room. Discuss what articles of furniture might be used to create a center of interest for emphasis. Remind them to allow a strip at the lower edge for a rug before drawing the shapes of the furniture against the wall. Suggest that the color scheme used include dark and grayed hues with just a touch of bright color for emphasis. Perhaps demonstrate how to paint clean edges by moving the whole arm, and dragging the edge of the brush against or along the line defining the shape on the paper.

EXPERIENCES WITH SPACE

"Big Pictures"

LEVEL 1

SUGGESTED MATERIALS: Paper at least 18″ × 24″, tempera paint, water pans, and brushes.

Discuss the concept of big and small with the class. A few children at this age might be able to understand that big things close by look smaller when they are at a distance. Most are not ready for this idea. Have each child think of something big enough to reach from the top to the bottom of his paper. Ask him to stretch his arms to show how big it will be. If the painting facilities are limited, freely brushing in the objects using black paint alone and later coloring with big wax crayons might be advisable. Encourage them to fill the entire paper.

Scenes with Multiple Base Lines

LEVEL 2

SUGGESTED MATERIALS: Flannel board, string, colored construction paper, sandpaper, and scissors.

Divide the flannel board horizontally with string lines to represent a near sidewalk, a street, and a far sidewalk. Discuss with the children the things that might be found in these areas. Ask them to cut these objects out of their construction paper. Supply a small piece of garnet sandpaper to paste on the back of each finished piece. Later have the children take turns creating a scene on the flannel board with their cutouts. This might culminate in a group mural of a street scene, or individual pictures.

Near-and-Far Scenes

LEVEL 3

See
ACTIVITY 24

SUGGESTED MATERIALS: Colored construction paper, scissors, paste, and possibly flannel board and garnet sandpaper.

Take the children to the best place available to observe that objects look proportionately bigger nearby and smaller far away. Let them observe the same phenomenon in pictures. Use cutouts and flannel-board manipulation, if necessary, to help them understand that near things are put lower on the picture surface as well as made proportionately larger. The class could then work either on individual paintings, or on a group mural. Country scenes are often the simplest for a first project using this concept. Do not be surprised if some children are not ready for a consistent application of this principle, however.

Overlapping Objects

LEVEL 4

See
ACTIVITY 24

SUGGESTED MATERIALS: Colored construction paper, scissors, paste, and possibly flannel board and garnet sandpaper.

Take the children to where there are good examples of overlapping objects of varied sizes. Examine pictures for further evidence of this phenomenon, and then put the pictures away and have children experiment with overlapping cutout objects either against a flannel board or at their desks. Call to their attention that objects seldom overlap on top of things lower on the picture surface. An exception would be objects flying in the air, such as birds. A forest scene made up of many overlapping trees might be the culmination of this activity.

Distance by Color Change

LEVEL 5

See
ACTIVITY 26

SUGGESTED MATERIALS: Boxes of semimoist water color, water pans, clean rags, brushes (No. 7 or larger), and paper 12″ × 18″.

Give the children opportunities to observe that color values change with distance, i.e., mountains turn purplish, and other colors are grayed or lightened. After outdoor observation, have the children observe the same effect in pictures. Demonstrate how adding water to the water color lightens it. Suggest simple water-color pictures in which a dark blue sky at the top of the paper fades into light nearer the horizon and green grass in the foreground fades into light in the distance. Encourage other experimentation to suggest distance, including placing objects such as trees in the landscape.

Painting "Space"

LEVEL 6

See
ACTIVITY 26

SUGGESTED MATERIALS: Boxes of semimoist water color, water pans, clean rags, brushes (No. 7 or larger), and paper 12″ × 18″.

Review with the class the concept that color value changes with distance. If possible, take the children to a place where they can observe the lines of railroad tracks or a road appearing to converge in the distance. This can be observed in pictures, but seeing it in actuality is better. Purely verbal explanations are the least satisfactory. Suggest that the children draw a winding road or river for emphasis against a background similar to that developed in the activity on Level 5. Some children will want to put objects on the road or river, letting them get tinier in the distance.

Linear Perspective

LEVEL 7

See
ACTIVITY 25

SUGGESTED MATERIALS: Cardboard about 6″ × 8″, scissors, drawing paper 9″ × 12″, pencils, and possibly paint that works easily on glass.

Show the children how to make "windows" about 4″ × 6″ in cardboard. Let them take these viewers outside so they can observe: (1) that two sides of a house are usually visible at a time, (2) that the base and roof lines of the house are seldom straight relative to the edges of the viewer, and (3) that horizontal lines above eye level appear to converge downward, while lines below eye level appear to converge upward. Later have them look at drawings and paintings using their viewers to observe convergence. Paint the lines of a building visible from the classroom with glass paint on a window. Some children need more evidence than others to clarify their understanding. Sketches of their own house, showing two sides, could be the culmination of this activity.

Emphasizing Form to Create Space

LEVEL 8

See
ACTIVITY 27

SUGGESTED MATERIALS: Cardboard about 6″ × 8″, scissors, drawing paper 9″ × 12″, and soft lead pencils.

Review with the students all the concepts they have learned on previous levels that enable them to create an illusion of space on a flat paper surface. Have them make viewer frames from cardboard and take the viewers outside so they can isolate one or two houses for careful study. Direct their attention to the fact that one side of the object is usually darker than the others. Dark edges against light exaggerate the feeling of form which creates an illusion of space flowing around the form. Some students might be ready to do a group of buildings in the medium of their choice as the culmination of this project. Others will not be able to go beyond pencil sketches.

EXPERIENCES WITH FORM

Papier-Mâché Modeling

LEVEL 1

See
ACTIVITY 43

SUGGESTED MATERIALS: Old newspapers, wheat flour, paste, water, a large container, and a stove.

Have the children tear newspaper into pieces about the size of a penny during their spare minutes. When the dish pan, or a similar container, is full, remove it to another area away from the children and follow the directions given in Activity 43. After the mixture has been prepared, give each child a small handful. Encourage them to squeeze and model it in their hands while the class discusses things to make. If it gets too dry, sprinkle it with water. Sometimes a little extra library paste helps a special part to stay together. When the objects are finished, allow them to dry for about a week in a warm, well-ventilated place. Color them with any available paint.

Cylindrical Masks

LEVEL 2

See
ACTIVITY 20

SUGGESTED MATERIALS: Colored construction paper 12″ × 18″, scissors, paste, and if possible a stapler.

Show children how to stretch a sheet of construction paper over a desk edge until it bends into cylinder form. Indicate how they are to fasten it. Discuss with them the different features that protrude from the head, and the methods that can be used to fasten things onto the cylinder, i.e., tabs, slitting, pasting, etc. Demonstrate how to fringe paper for hair or eyelashes. Suggest hats for the masks if they have time. Establish a central table or box for the exchange of usable scraps.

Cylinder Creatures

LEVEL 3

See
ACTIVITY 21

SUGGESTED MATERIALS: Colored construction material, scissors, paste, and if possible a stapler.

Discuss with the children the similarity of their arms, legs, and trunk to cylinders. Show them how they can stretch a piece of construction paper across the edge of their desk until it bends into cylinder form. Demonstrate how little tabs can be left along the edges to fasten the parts together. Small cylinders can be formed by rolling paper around pencils. Suggest that animals, totem poles, and katcina dolls as well as people can be made from cylinders. Encourage imaginative solutions to the project.

Paper Hats

LEVEL 4

See
ACTIVITY 18

SUGGESTED MATERIALS: Colored construction paper 12″ × 18″, scissors, paste, and if possible a stapler.

Review with the class all the ways they have learned to manipulate paper on previous levels. Direct the preparation of 12″ × 18″ construction paper by cutting 4″ diagonals from each corner and 4″ cuts at right angles to the edge, halfway down each long side. Arouse enthusiasm for twisting and fastening the paper in various ways to make an imaginative hat. A mirror to view the results is helpful. Encourage children to add the paper decoration needed for a gay effect.

Conical Creations

LEVEL 5

See
ACTIVITY 19

SUGGESTED MATERIALS: Colored construction paper, scissors, paste, compasses, pins, and if possible a stapler.

Lead a class discussion about things that are cone-shaped. Furnish compasses to draw circles on construction paper. Remind the children that paper is easier to manipulate after being stretched over a desk edge. Show how cutting wedged-shaped pieces of different sizes out of circles will make cones of different heights. Pinning the cone together with straight pins will be helpful until the paste dries. Encourage imaginative combinations of cones and cylinders.

Dioramas

LEVEL 6

SUGGESTED MATERIALS: Shoe boxes, construction paper, scissors, paste, and odds and ends such as pipe-cleaners.

See
Activity 23 Direct discussion of the diorama as a three-dimensional scene set up in a box with one side open for viewing. Stress the similarity to a miniature stage. Encourage experimentation with various methods for making figures, trees, and animals in three dimensions. Paper may be used, although children should feel free to use other materials. Pipe-cleaners, for example, can be easily bent to form creatures of various sorts. Emphasize the need for a center of interest.

Posters

LEVEL 7

See
Activity 22

SUGGESTED MATERIALS: Colored construction paper 12″ × 18″, rulers, scissors, and paste.

Discuss with the students the premise that the first objective in planning a poster is to catch the onlooker's attention; the second, to tell him something important. Explore with them the possibilities of a simple word, such as "STOP," as a heading for a poster. Suggest that the illustration of the message should be in three dimensions, fastened onto the 12″ × 18″ sheet of construction paper. For example show "STOP" above, and a fire below, made by rolling brown paper logs and twisting orange paper flames. Encourage diversity.

Sculptural Form

LEVEL 8

See
Activity 9

SUGGESTED MATERIALS: Plaster, vermiculite, cement, stiff paper, metal findings, soap, papier-mâché, soft wood, etc.

Examine with the class the work of modern sculptors, such as Brancusi, who create forms that are not easily identified as real objects. Direct a class discussion toward the discovery that forms can have good design in terms of continuity, emphasis, and balance without realism. Explore the materials that can be used for sculpture. A committee could be given this assignment. Later discuss the materials available, and let the choice of materials be an individual one, as far as possible.

SECTION TWO

Using People in Elementary-School Art

OBJECTIVES

To provide technical means that simplify the problems of including people in art expression.

To encourage children to use people frequently in their art work by suggesting stimulating ideas.

To sharpen children's perceptions of the human figure at rest and in action.

There are four suggestions for using people on each of the eight levels below. The challenging activities are planned to appeal to a child at that level, and to free him from some of his fears of using people in art. Projects for older students are planned to allow for the self-consciousness of the adolescent. The teacher's confidence and enthusiasm will be reflected in the children's work.

Many People

LEVEL I

SUGGESTED MATERIALS: Newsprint 18″ × 24″, black tempera paint, and brushes. Crayons can be substituted, but they lack the freedom of paint.

Plan carefully the distribution of supplies and the best places for the children to work, if this is their first experience with paint. Protect the desk or table surfaces with newspaper, and show them how to wipe excess paint off brushes to help prevent dripping. When all is ready, present the challenge, "See how many people you can get on your paper!" Make it seem exciting. At this stage there should be no attempt to define how a person looks. Many children will not be ready to paint recognizable figures. However, people are very important in their lives. Let their exuberant expression be recognized. Colors can be painted or crayoned in later if the children's interest is sustained.

Pale Pink People

LEVEL I

See
ACTIVITY 31

SUGGESTED MATERIALS: Newsprint 18″ × 24″, assorted tempera paint, including flesh color, brushes, and if necessary crayon.

Have different children demonstrate how their arms and legs bend at the elbow and knee. Note that the arm starts up at the shoulder. Some children will be ready to use this information, others will not. Distribute supplies, but include only the flesh-colored paint at this time. Develop enthusiasm in the children for filling the paper with many pale pink people. As the children finish the first challenge, put out other colors for clothes to dress up the people. It is best to have a separate brush for each color, and to ask the children to keep the brushes in the same color. If this is impossible, teach the children to clean the brushes in water jars. Do not expect all the children to depict real people at this stage.

Family Faces

LEVEL 1

See
ACTIVITY 28

SUGGESTED MATERIALS: Newsprint 18″ × 24″, assorted tempera paint, including flesh color, and if necessary crayon.

Talk about the shape of heads. Help the children to see the front of the head as an oval with hair on top and the facial features below. Encourage them to paint a big oval of flesh-colored paint to represent each member of their family. Distribute other colors so that they can paint hair on top of the ovals, and the other features below. Have boys stand up to call attention to their ears as a distinguishing feature. Remark on the variety of length and style found in the hair of women and girls. Some children will be ready to add details of clothing, others will scarcely produce recognizable faces.

Clay People

LEVEL 1

SUGGESTED MATERIALS: Clay or Plasticene and a protected surface to work on.

Encourage the children to manipulate clay until it is responsive. Talk about the way arms and legs grow out of the body. Show them how they can pinch, poke, and pull to make the head, arms, and legs. Make the demonstration a casual affair. Put the emphasis on their "growing" people with head, arms, legs, and maybe hands and feet. Express enthusiasm about the evolving "people." Do not be surprised if many children simply manipulate the clay. Accept every child's work, but do not feel obligated to preserve everything. Children can understand that clay must be saved to use another day.

Helpers

LEVEL 2

See
ACTIVITY 32

SUGGESTED MATERIALS: Newsprint 18″ × 24″, assorted tempera paint, including flesh color, brushes, and, if needed, water pans. Crayons can be used if paints are not available.

Discuss with the children the various workers who do things for us. Distribute the supplies. Ask the children to show with their hands how "tall" their paper is. Challenge them to make their favorite helpers so big and strong that their heads will touch the top of the paper and their feet the bottom. Help the children to think about the other things they can put in their pictures to show where their helpers work and what they work with. Encourage the children to fill up the paper, although some of them will not be ready for this challenge.

Playground Scenes

LEVEL 2

See
ACTIVITY 31

SUGGESTED MATERIALS: Manila paper 12″ × 18″ and assorted wax crayons, including pieces of orange crayon about ½″ long.

Have the class pause during playground play and direct their attention to all the activity around them. Continue the discussion later, after the supplies have been given out. Show them briefly how the sides of chalk or crayon can be used to make lively action figures, but do not have your examples in evidence while the children are working. Suggest that clothes can be put on top of the orange crayon easily with bright colors of wax crayon. Be enthusiastic about having many people in their playground pictures, without rushing those who work at a slower pace. Those who finish first might like to start a large playground mural to which the others can contribute later. Encourage really big figures (8″ to 10″ tall) on the large paper.

Many Faces

LEVEL 2

See
ACTIVITY 28

SUGGESTED MATERIALS: Manila paper 12″ × 18″ and assorted wax crayons or tempera paint and brushes.

Discuss times and places where the members of the class have seen large numbers of people. Review, by directed observation, the basic oval of the human face. Speculate, with the children, about how many ovals they can place on a sheet of paper using either flesh-colored tempera paint or orange wax crayon. Ask them how they can make the ovals all into "different" people. Emphasize the features people have in common as well as individual variations in color and shape. Expect a wide range in the ability of the children to use detail.

Little Clay People

LEVEL 2

See
ACTIVITY 69

SUGGESTED MATERIALS: Clay or Plasticene and a protected surface to work on.

While the children are manipulating the clay, discuss with them the resemblance of their own arms and legs to the cylinders they like to roll. Suggest that they can have fun making little clay people if they fasten clay arms and legs firmly to the bodies. Show them dramatically what happens when clay pieces are not pressed firmly together. This is particularly important if you are using water-base clay that will later be fired in a kiln. Parts are likely to fall off during the preliminary drying, or later during the actual firing, if they have not been carefully put together.

Rainy-Day Clothes

LEVEL 3

See
ACTIVITY 32

SUGGESTED MATERIALS: Manila or gray paper 12″ × 18″ and assorted wax crayons or tempera paint and brushes.

Wait for a rainy day to begin a class discussion of what boys and girls need to wear for adequate protection outdoors. Challenge the children to make a single figure dressed for a rainy day, big enough to touch the top and bottom of their paper held the long way. Umbrellas over the figure's head can be used to help reach the top. Later suggest that any empty spaces on the paper might be used to indicate wet surroundings. Show enthusiasm for puddles and similar details.

Happy Faces

LEVEL 3

See
ACTIVITY 34

SUGGESTED MATERIALS: Manila paper 12″ × 18″ and chalk, wax crayon, or tempera paint and brushes.

Guide a class discussion of happy times into an analysis of how a person's face shows that he is happy. The mouth turning up at the ends will probably be mentioned along with other indications. Have a brief review of the colored oval as a base on which facial features are distributed. Consider whether the class is ready to use the eyes midway down the oval as an orientation for the other features. Get the children to make the faces large (6″ to 8″), so that they can be seen from across the room.

Crowds of People

LEVEL 3

See
ACTIVITY 31

SUGGESTED MATERIALS: Manila paper 12″ × 18″ and assorted wax crayons or tempera paint and brushes.

Distribute supplies, and then guide a discussion to crowds the children have been in. This activity might be used at a time when some local happening has made the experience recent and real. Review the simple method of creating people in action by using the side of a crayon or colored tempera paint to make arms, legs, trunk, and head. Arrive at a group consensus as to how many people they must have on their papers before they can say they have made a crowd (five might be a minimum). Encourage enough background to communicate where the action takes place.

Clay Clowns

LEVEL 3

See
ACTIVITY 69

SUGGESTED MATERIALS: Clay or Plasticene, a protected surface to work on, and tongue blades.

Use stimuli to start a class discussion of circuses, specifically clowns. The best stimulation, of course, is a recent visit to a circus, but children will probably have seen clowns or other circus acts on television. Discuss the facial exaggerations that are typical of a clown. Point out that the wooden blade can be helpful in modeling the clay and poking it into shape. Let the children decide whether they want to make just a clown's head or a whole clown, complete with funny clothes, Review the necessity for attaching extra pieces of clay firmly to the body. Clay objects can be gayly painted or glazed after they have thoroughly dried. Tempera paint can be given a coat of clear lacquer or shellac for protection.

Parades

LEVEL 4

See
ACTIVITY 31

SUGGESTED MATERIALS: Manila paper 12″ × 18″ and assorted crayons or tempera paint and brushes.

Recall, with the children, the excitement of a parade. Perhaps, after the supplies have been distributed, take time for a march around the room to music. Review the use of the side of a short piece of crayon to make arms and legs in action. Discuss the background behind the marching people. The buildings of a city street could be suggested, or the trees and houses of a small town. Flags and airplanes can be added to fill any empty spaces. Emphasize the color of parades. If tempera paint is used, encourage the children to cover every bit of the paper with paint.

Sad People

LEVEL 4

See
ACTIVITY 34

SUGGESTED MATERIALS: Manila paper 12″ × 18″ and chalk, crayon, or tempera paint and brushes.

Discuss with the class the changes in features that make a face look sad. Have one or two demonstrations, taking care that the children do not lapse into silliness. Distribute the supplies. Focus attention on having the eyes halfway from the top to the bottom of the head, as an orientation to help in locating the other features. Since this project presumes prior experience in drawing faces on previous levels, review any needed items from those activities. Accept each student's work on its own level.

Unusual Costumes

LEVEL 4

See
ACTIVITY 29

SUGGESTED MATERIALS: Colored or Manila paper 12″ × 18″ and chalk, assorted wax crayons, or tempera paint and brushes.

Present this project at a time relevant to Halloween, Mardi gras, or when a class begins to be too concerned about realism in art. Emphasize that although they start with a human face everything else is imaginary. Repeat frequently that the costume should be unlike any the children have ever seen before. When they are well started, wander around and praise the fantastic ideas that are evolving.

Clay People in "Action"

LEVEL 4

See
ACTIVITY 69

SUGGESTED MATERIALS: Clay or Plasticene, a protected surface to work on, and sticks or clay-modeling tools.

Review prior experiences the children have had in modeling clay people. Suggest that now they are old enough not only to fasten arms, legs, and heads on securely, but to make their people walk! Have one child at a time walk across the room while the others examine which way the body, arms, and legs bend. Guide their observation with questions such as, "Is the body straight as a telegraph pole when a person walks, or does it bend forward?" The development of perceptual awareness is more important than the finished project which may or may not be preserved.

People Playing

LEVEL 5

See
ACTIVITY 31

SUGGESTED MATERIALS: Assorted colored paper, including light orange or flesh-colored, background sheets 12″ × 18″ or larger, scissors, and paste.

Recall the clay people made on the fourth level. Direct the children's observation to the fact that invariably when people are active their arms and legs are bent, and demonstrate how the limbs can be cut from colored paper. The pieces of paper should be the length of an arm or a leg and bent to a slight angle in the middle. When the people are assembled and clothed, they can be shown playing various games. Discourage drawing first with a pencil. Emphasize the fun of assembling many people and pasting them to the background sheet. Be prepared for considerable distortion, but much vitality.

Favorite Shirts or Blouses

LEVEL 5

SUGGESTED MATERIALS: Colored or Manila paper 12″ × 18″ and assorted wax crayons, including small odd pieces.

Direct the attention of the children to the variety of colors, designs, and other details to be found among the blouses and shirts worn by members of the class. Show them how stripes and plaids can be simply made by using the sides of small pieces of crayon. Discuss favorite shirts and blouses. Suggest that if they have no particular favorite among their clothes they might design one to suit them. Leave the matter of including heads and other parts of the body up to the individuals.

Cylindrical People

LEVEL 5

See
ACTIVITY 21

SUGGESTED MATERIALS: Colored construction paper, paste, scissors, and a stapler if available.

Wait until there is a need for some three-dimensional figures, perhaps in a display or poster, and then introduce the idea of making them from paper. Remind the children that construction paper can be made more flexible by stretching it over the edge of a desk or table. Small cylinders can be rolled around pencils for tiny arms and legs. It is possible to cut a slit on the inside of an arm to make it bend at the elbow. Praise ingenuity in making paper people.

Self-Portraits

LEVEL 5

See
ACTIVITY 28

SUGGESTED MATERIALS: Manila paper 12″ × 18″ and assorted chalk or wax crayons.

Begin a discussion of individual differences in hair and eye coloring or other facial features. Introduce the idea of making a picture of oneself. Remind children of their numerous previous experiences in making faces on earlier levels, and review what they learned then. Place a mirror or two away from the working area for children to take turns at later, when they feel a need to check on details. If the children are beginning to be quite self-conscious, restrict their examination of each other's drawings.

People from Another Planet

LEVEL 6

See
ACTIVITY 33

SUGGESTED MATERIALS: Manila or white drawing paper 12″ × 18″, assorted wax crayons, water-color boxes, brushes, and water pans.

Direct the class discussion toward the possibility of life on another planet. Stimulate their imagination until they are considering the possible variations in size, shape, and color of living creatures in an entirely different environment from that on earth. Suggest that they draw both the "people" and their surroundings with heavy pressure on their wax crayon. The strange atmosphere of another planet can be indicated by brushing water color over the entire paper. If the wax crayon is thick enough, it will resist the paint.

Fun Together

LEVEL 6

See
ACTIVITY 45

SUGGESTED MATERIALS: Background paper 18″ × 24″ or larger (depending on the number in each group), assorted colored paper, scissors, and paste.

Divide the class into compatible groups of three or more children. Guide a discussion into the wide variety of recreation available for people today. Suggest that each group choose a different activity to illustrate against an appropriate background. Designate a place to sign up for exclusive rights to a specific type of recreation. Review the simple approach to creating active cut-paper figures used on the fifth level. Praise ingenuity and evidence of good cooperative effort.

Solid Faces

LEVEL 6

See
ACTIVITY 30

SUGGESTED MATERIALS: Manila paper 12″ × 18″ and assorted wax crayons or chalk.

Review previous experiences in drawing faces. Guide a class discussion toward discovering how drawings of heads can be made to look less flat, and more like solid forms. Direct the children's observation to places where shadows are most noticeable—around the eyes, along the side of the nose, between the lips, and around the edges of the face. Have them feel their own faces, particularly their noses. Encourage them to use the side of a dark crayon to give a feeling of form to the flat, colored oval of the face.

Near and Far Away

LEVEL 6

See
ACTIVITY 24

SUGGESTED MATERIALS: Manila paper 12″ × 18″ and chalk, wax crayons, or tempera paint and brushes.

Plan to do this at some time after the children have completed the sixth level project on page 98. Explain that they are to imagine themselves standing at the lower edge of their page waving to a tiny figure of a friend away up a winding road. To draw this picture the children must understand many concepts previously explained on page 30. (Some children will not be ready to use all the information they have been exposed to.) Encourage them to add details such as trees and grass in the pictures.

Sketching Faces

LEVEL 7

See
ACTIVITY 30

SUGGESTED MATERIALS: Plenty of Manila paper or newsprint 9″ × 12″ and chalk, charcoal, or small pieces of wax crayons.

Distribute the supplies, giving each student several sheets of paper. Review the concepts they learned on previous levels, particularly the orientation of the other features to the placement of the eyes midway on the oval representing the face. Mention that the nose usually ends halfway from the eyes to the chin. Emphasize, though, that individuals differ, and that is what makes sketching faces fun. Allow five to eight minutes for each sketch made of a neighbor's face. Minimize silliness, which is likely to be troublesome at this self-conscious age, by making the showing or preservation of the sketches optional.

Skating Figures

LEVEL 7

See
ACTIVITY 31

SUGGESTED MATERIALS: Manila paper 12″ × 18″ and assorted wax crayons or water-color boxes with brushes and water pans.

Discuss the lively action to be found on the local skating rink. Suggest using either the side of a short piece of orange crayon or a brush and pale orange paint, to establish the people skating. Consider forbidding the use of pencil, since at this age it is almost always inhibiting to the drawing of figures in action. Emphasize as the projects progress that plenty of bright colors will make the scene look gay and lively.

Quaint Costumes

LEVEL 7

SUGGESTED MATERIALS: White or other drawing paper 9″ × 12″, wax crayons, paint, brushes, and water pans.

Exhibit pictures of peasant costumes and guide students' enjoyment of their color and imaginative detail. Tell them that this type of clothing is fast disappearing. Since peasant outfits were homemade, suggest that the students will enjoy designing costumes for themselves. Permit them to borrow ideas for small details from the pictures, but keep the resource material away from the working area. Emphasize that the end result should be unlike any known peasant costume. If uniformity in size (as for an exhibit) is important, suggest that the figures be made 8″ tall, including 1″ heads.

Three-Dimensional Action Figures

LEVEL 7

See
ACTIVITY 21

SUGGESTED MATERIALS: Colored construction paper, scissors, paste, and if possible a stapler.

Wait for an occasion when there is a need for three-dimensional paper figures for an exhibit, decorations, or perhaps for posters. Review with the students the stretching and fastening procedures they learned at earlier levels when making cylinder people. Suggest experimentation with slits at the elbows and knees to allow the figures to appear active. Encourage ingenuity in making devices to enable the people to stand up. Probably the simplest device is to fasten paper feet to the end of the legs, and then secure the feet in walking position to a piece of cardboard.

Clay Heads

LEVEL 8

SUGGESTED MATERIALS: Clay or Plasticene, sticks or modeling tools, and protected surface to work on.

Discuss the basic shape of the head as the students manipulate the clay to give it pliability. Help them to become aware of the indentations and projecting forms of the face by feeling their own. Review the approximate position of the various features from work on previous levels. Encourage the students to model the head and major features rapidly before spending time on details such as the texture of the hair. The preservation of the heads is relatively unimportant to the learning process and should be dependent on local facilities for glazing and firing.

Sketching People

LEVEL 8

See
ACTIVITY 35

SUGGESTED MATERIALS: Plenty of Manila paper or newsprint 12″ × 18″ and chalk, charcoal, a felt-tip pen or small pieces of wax crayon.

Borrow a child or two from a primary grade if the students are likely to feel self-conscious about posing for five-minute sketches. Emphasize that quickly placing long, action lines lightly on the paper will help the details to line up correctly later. Discourage any use of pencil unless very soft primary pencils can be borrowed. Minimize the comparing of drawings, and consider letting students discard their sketches at the end of the time.

Designing Clothes

LEVEL 8

SUGGESTED MATERIALS: White Bond typing or tracing paper and wax crayons or colored pencils.

Spend some time in a class discussion of appropriate, good-looking clothes for various occasions. Suggest that the students probably have wished at times that they could buy a complete outfit of their own choice. Present them with the opportunity to design clothes for themselves. Offer several outline sketches of teen-agers to students who hesitate to draw figures on their own. Mention that you are allowing them this crutch because the emphasis is on creating an original outfit in a choice of favorite colors.

Twenty-First-Century People

LEVEL **8**

SUGGESTED MATERIALS: Drawing paper 12″ × 18″ and a choice of available media.

See
ACTIVITY 33

Focus the attention of the class on the people of the next century and their possible environment. Challenge them to interpret the future each in his own way with the one stipulation that they include people. Encourage them to sketch lightly (perhaps with white chalk) until they have planned something for every part of the paper including the sky. They can work out the details later. This procedure will help them overcome the tendency students at this age have to develop one small area completely while neglecting the rest of the picture.

SECTION THREE

Using Subjective Experiences in Elementary-School Art

OBJECTIVES

To create an awareness that art is essentially a means of expressing the artist's reaction to his environment.

To supply each student with sufficient stimulation to make him feel he wants to make his picture something very personal; something uniquely expressive of himself.

To utilize every available means of creating an atmosphere during the art activities that will free each child to express himself. Some suggestions:

1. Background music
2. Positive criticism
3. Choice of medium
4. Choice of paper
5. Praise for individuality
6. Freedom to start over if not satisfied
7. Freedom to ignore the subject suggested if a more exciting idea comes to mind
8. Freedom to call work finished when the child feels satisfied.

Most of the activities on the other continuums for elementary school art are planned to develop facility with the tools and materials of visual communication. There are long-term goals: a sense of this year's work building on that of last year. The children develop a feeling of competency in art which should give them the confidence to continue their interest into adulthood.

It is very important to this continued growth that the children on every level understand that all art is not concerned with reproducing accurately the appearance of things. Children of every age should have frequent, probably weekly, opportunities to express how they feel about the world of people and nature in which they live. In many schools the only art goal is the free expression of the children's experiences. This has proven inadequate by itself beyond the primary grades, except for a few gifted individuals. The real need is for a well-balanced approach to creative art.

An art period devoted to subjective or personal expression by the children requires careful planning by the teacher if impoverished stereotypes are to be avoided. A new medium, or a combination of materials and techniques suggested for section III in Part One, often proves stimulating.

Sometimes a change of pace is needed. There should occasionally be quick, fifteen-minute opportunities for art expression, perhaps in chalk. As children grow older, they can benefit by spending several twenty-minute periods on a single project, perhaps once a month. The immaturity of much children's art work is simply evidence of a habit of devoting little time and energy to the subject. The children should understand in advance that the activity will be worked on over a period of time. The first day probably would be devoted to lightly sketching in the complete project and indicating the large areas of color throughout. The second day might be spent on developing the details, particularly in the center of interest. The third day could be devoted to evaluating and improving the over-all design after considering its balance, continuity, and emphasis. The total time expended need not be more than an hour, but with the diversified emphases a richer experience is possible for each child.

Another reason the self-expression of many children is impoverished and repetitive is found in a lack of stimuli. The boxlike house and the lollypop tree are symbols of the uninspired and the unperceptive. Any one of the sentences below can be used as a basis for group discussion bringing out the wide range of visual possibilities that can be developed from each suggestion. A sensitive teacher will know when sufficient stimulation has been given. At that time most children will be eager to get to work. It is suggested that only one sentence be developed at any one time for stimulation in "depth." The teacher should be receptive to deviations from the suggested experience. The imaginative child should be encouraged to do things his own way. The unimaginative should be given additional, individualized stimuli after the others have begun.

Suggested Stimuli
for Recalling Subjective Experiences

LEVEL 1
He was the funniest clown.
It was a dreary, rainy night.
There wasn't a house in sight.
This is the pet that I would like most to have.

LEVEL 2
I had a bad dream.
I was all alone.
There was an old, old house in the woods.
The fire was warm and cozy.

LEVEL 3
I was frightened.
It was very dark outside.
I think that would be the most fun in the world.
This is my favorite toy.

LEVEL 4
I was lost in the woods.
I climbed the highest place in the world.
This is from my favorite television program (or movie).
The wind nearly blew me away.

LEVEL 5
Something was chasing me.
It was a beautiful sunset.
We went camping.
I dreamed I was king (or queen).

LEVEL 6
I was lost in a big city.
This was my favorite holiday.
This is my own castle.
It was a gray, snowy day.

LEVEL 7
I met a creature from another planet.
It was a terrible storm.
This is the house I would like to live in.
I would like very much to visit this place.

LEVEL 8
I felt myself suddenly becoming very ugly.
No one would recognize me in this costume.
Suddenly there was an earthquake.
I woke up in 2050 A.D.

SECTION FOUR

Correlating Art and Other Subjects

TO THE TEACHER

When correlating art with other subject-matter areas, each teacher should ask himself the following questions:

    1. Does my class have sufficient background in this topic so that we can put away reference material once the art activity is begun? (Carefully controlled access might be provided once the project is well under way, but no student should work with reference material in front of him.)

    2. Can I justify spending the time needed to complete the project in terms of the growth the child will attain in art and the other subject?

If the project chosen has no possibilities for creative planning and individual variations in the finished product, DON'T CALL IT ART, and don't use it as a substitute for a creative art activity. If it seems to be a very valuable activity, despite its lack of creativity, let the time spent come within the period ordinarily spent on the subject to which it pertains. The suggested subject matter in this section may have to be adapted to fit into the local curriculum.

Number Booklet

LEVEL I

SUGGESTED MATERIALS: Carrots, dull paring knives or similar tools, newsprint (tinted if available), old newspapers, tempera paint, a stapler, and heavier paper for covers.

Plan this activity for any time when the children need a quick, enjoyable way to visualize numbers. Have the children cover their working space with newspaper. Distribute at least half a carrot to each child. Show them how their tools can be used to cut a design into the wide flat end. Demonstrate, making a printing pad from 12 to 20 pieces of newspaper about 6" × 6" placed one on top of the other and thoroughly dampened. Place a spoonful of tempera paint on the pad and press the end of the carrot onto it. Print the carrot design on newsprint. Once the children have experimented with the process, explain the arithmetic problems they are to visualize. Staple pages together for a booklet. The cover can be heavier paper covered with printed reproductions of the designs.

"Our Houses"

LEVEL I

SUGGESTED MATERIALS: Assorted colored construction paper, background paper about 24" × 60" or larger, paste, pins, and scissors.

See
ACTIVITY 46

Discuss the colors and other distinctive characteristics of the houses within view of the classroom windows. Ask each child to close his eyes and remember the colors and other details of his own house. Give him the opportunity to choose construction paper nearest the remembered colors. Encourage many details by questions, but do not expect great skill in depiction. Assemble houses by rows on background paper, using pins. Before pasting them, consider rearranging them to place the largest houses on the bottom row, with some overlapping in subsequent rows.

Neighborhood Picture Map

LEVEL 1

See
ACTIVITY 47

SUGGESTED MATERIALS: Newsprint or Manila drawing paper 9″ × 12″, background paper 48″ × 48″ if possible, crayons, scissors, and paste.

Prepare large paper with a simplified map of streets around the school, making the streets about 1″ wide. The school site might be the center of orientation. Take the children on a walk, after their first view of the map, to look for things to put on it. If this is their first experience with a map, have them draw, color, and cut out what they want to put on it from small paper. Encourage them to pin, rather than paste, onto the big paper until there is time for a class discussion to ensure that things are where the class means them to be. Do not expect great accuracy. A more experienced group might take turns drawing or painting directly on the big map.

Safety Posters

LEVEL 1

See
ACTIVITY 22

SUGGESTED MATERIALS: Bright, light-colored construction paper 12″ × 18″ and crayons.

Talk with the children about dangerous situations they have seen. Direct their attention to additional hazardous actions that children should avoid for safety reasons. Ask each child to choose one dangerous activity to draw large, with bright colors on his paper. Discuss the meaning of red in stop signals. Suggest to the children that they use red crayons to print "S T O P" in big letters in an empty place on their papers.

Sentence Storybook

LEVEL 2

SUGGESTED MATERIALS: Newsprint manufactured with lines below and space for picture above, or facsimiles from newsprint 12″ × 18″, crayons, heavy paper or cardboard for covers, and paper fasteners or rings.

Plan this as a continuing project to be started as soon as children have a primer-level vocabulary. Some children can continue it independently as an enrichment activity. At first help the children think through the problem of communicating to others. Give them pride in their original ideas. A story without an ending might be used to inspire their first efforts, their pictures and sentences telling what they think happened next. Praise and enthusiasm will make them want to do more pages for their book. At any time the papers can be collected between covers, decorated, and fastened to make a book.

Safety on the Playground

LEVEL 2

See
ACTIVITY 45

SUGGESTED MATERIALS: Two lengths of project roll or paper 3′ × 4′ and crayons or tempera paint with brushes.

Discuss with the children the dangerous activities they have seen on the local playground. Divide the class into two groups (by free choice if possible). One group will create a safe playground on their large sheet. The others will draw their scene with children doing dangerous things. Demonstrate drawing people in action with the side of a short orange crayon, or with pale orange paint. Decide, by group discussion, on a height for the children on the playgrounds—possibly 6″. Arrange that no more than four children are working on one sheet at a time. Later, decide with the class whether background color is needed in the empty spaces.

Local Transportation

LEVEL 2

See
ACTIVITY 46

SUGGESTED MATERIALS: A length of project roll or 3′ × 4′ paper for background, colored paper, scissors, and paste.

Lead the class to decide what local methods of transportation they want to feature in their mural. If there is a body of water, it might be placed low on the paper, with possibly a train above, a highway nearby and planes in the sky. Either help the students to divide into groups, each specializing in cutting out one type of vehicle, or have each child make a variety over a period of days. Some children might want to make buildings for background. Assemble the objects with pins and let the group decide on the placement of them before pasting them permanently.

Farm Animals

LEVEL 2

SUGGESTED MATERIALS: A wooden sawhorse, scraps of 2″ × 4″ wood, newspapers, string, scissors, nails, a hammer, a stapler, brown paper tape, water glass (sodium silicate), brushes, and tempera paint.

Guide the children in a study of the unique characteristics of the animal they want to make. Obtain a sawhorse and decide as a group on the length and proper angle of the pieces of wood to be nailed onto it to form the skeleton of a neck and head. Form a group to tie and staple big balls of crumpled newspaper onto the wooden frame for bulk. When it is well padded, have another group work together to brush a mixture of half water glass and half water onto full sheets of newspaper. Place the sheets over the crumpled newspaper and shape them to the contours of the animal. Use brown paper tape on loose edges. The surface will be quite rigid and not easily damaged when it is thoroughly dry. Paint it with tempera.

Little Book of Illustrated Stories

LEVEL 3

SUGGESTED MATERIALS: Special paper made with space for pictures above the lines (or alternate sheets of writing paper and drawing paper of the same size), crayons, heavier paper for covers, and paper fasteners or rings.

Help the children develop both visual and verbal ability by having them create their own books. A group discussion of ideas might provide the impetus for their first work. Interest and enthusiasm grows with encouragement from the teacher. Sometimes a drawing will inspire a story. At other times the story will be written first. In either case the impetus comes from "making something happen" to characters. Originality should be the prime criterion.

Hand Puppets of Story Characters

LEVEL 3

See
ACTIVITY 44

SUGGESTED MATERIALS: Colored lunch bags about 10″ long, scraps of colored construction paper, scissors, and paste.

Guide the children in their reading groups to decide what stories they want to act out with hand puppets. Show them how the hand inside the bag can grip the fold near the bottom. Then by opening and closing the hand the "mouth" of the puppet is created on the exterior. The characters are indicated by pasting on features of colored paper and any other appropriate materials. After casts of characters made this way have been used, they can be stored in a large bag and brought out for action on another day.

Picture Map of County Landmarks

LEVEL 3

See
ACTIVITY 47

SUGGESTED MATERIALS: A dittoed map of a route taken on a bus trip to various county landmarks, Manila paper 9" × 12", crayons, scissors, paste, and background paper 3' × 4'.

After a class discussion of places in the county to be visited, prepare a ditto map of a route. Actually following this route makes their map more meaningful. Sharpen the children's perception of colors and details by questions at the various landmarks. The following day guide a discussion that will recall these characteristics before the children begin their crayon drawings. Show appreciation of those children who remember special details. The time available should determine whether all the children draw every scene for individual maps or contribute to a large map of the county.

Music Murals

LEVEL 3

See
ACTIVITY 5

SUGGESTED MATERIALS: Paper 3' × 4' (smaller sheets can be pasted together), chalk in assorted colors, prepared liquid starch, a spray gun, and water pans.

Divide the class so that children are working together in groups of about four on the floor or at a table. Show how dipping the chalk quickly in water before using it cuts down on chalk dust. Have the class listen to the music a bit, and then have each group choose one member to create a big swinging line that dominates the paper and sets the rhythm. Have other members join in until the entire paper is covered with lines and color areas suggested by the music. Try spraying the finished projects with a mixture of three parts water to one of starch to protect them from smudging.

"Our State" Booklet

LEVEL 4

See
ACTIVITY 48

SUGGESTED MATERIALS: Drawing paper the size of the proposed booklet, heavier paper for a cover, paper fasteners, and crayons.

Select the simpler, more distinctive points of interest in the state for a book. Do only one at a time, and do not let work on it substitute for the regular art period. The last portion of the social studies time is more appropriate. Show several views of the landmark or area being studied. By questioning, call the children's attention to the general shape and color of things and the important details. Put all pictures on a remote table before the class starts working. (But if, near the conclusion of his work, a child wishes to look again at a picture *away from his work*, there is no harm in allowing him to do so.) Adopt a lighthearted, "draw what you remember" approach. Never use negative criticism, and show delight when children include special details.

Pioneer Buildings of the State

LEVEL 4

See
ACTIVITY 49

SUGGESTED MATERIALS: Miscellaneous boxes, cardboard, colored construction paper, scissors, and paste.

Guide the children in forming committees to construct old-time buildings out of cardboard. Demonstrate the use of a box or boxes for the basic shape of a building with the facade, roof, and other details added by cutting and pasting. Sometimes the plans of the various groups can be coordinated to form a village with miniature people. Construction paper spread on a table top makes a simple base. Do not spend more time than necessary on the project, since it has limited creative possibilities.

Indian-Life Mural

LEVEL 4

See
ACTIVITY 45

SUGGESTED MATERIALS: Background paper about 3′ × 5′, tempera paint, sponges, and brushes.

Following a considerable study of the territories of Indian tribes, lead a class discussion during which the children contribute to a list of all the things typical of life in those tribes. Decide as a group what aspect of their life to feature. Have the class elect a committee to write in lightly on the background paper where various Indian activities might be placed. When their work is completed, hold another class discussion on whether the important things are emphasized. Plan painting participation. First a committee might use small sponges to daub in the background. Others make their contribution in turn. The Indian figures can be painted directly with reddish brown paint for more feeling of action.

Maps of the State

LEVEL 4

SUGGESTED MATERIALS vary with choice of activity and are included below.

Maps to be of value should present accurate concepts. This limits their value as an art project, and the time spent on them should be taken from the social studies period in most cases. Here are some suggestions: Use chalk to sketch, with the help of the children, a large map of the state on the playground pavement. Locate the principal cities by drawing small circles. Use the map to play a game of aiming a flat "skipper" from one city to the next over a designated route.
Create individual picture maps similar to the group map on level 3.
After studying topography, use cooked papier-mâché pulp (see Part One, Activity 43) to create contours of the state on a firm base of masonite or wood. Paint the map later with tempera paint.

Fraction Booklets

LEVEL 5

See
ACTIVITY 22

SUGGESTED MATERIALS: Assorted colors of 9″ × 12″ poster or construction paper, scissors, rulers, compasses, paste, and paper fasteners.

During an arithmetic period show the children how to draw circles on their colored paper, then divide the circles into wedge-shaped pieces of different fractional proportions. Although this activity is not creative, the lettering for the cover can be artful. Bring before the class examples of legible, but imaginative, lettering from magazines and advertisements. Ask the children to look for other examples. Let them cut strips of colored paper in two heights, one for the tall letters and the other for the shorter letters. Have them draw the letters they need lightly with pencil in a style imaginatively adapted from the numerous examples they have seen. Stress the need to make the letters appear to be an equal distance apart on the booklet cover, with wider spaces between words. Irregularities in width, or even in height, should not be considered too important.

Picture Map of Western Trails

LEVEL 5

See
ACTIVITY 47

SUGGESTED MATERIALS: Large 3′ × 4′ paper with an outline of the western half of the United States and crayons or water colors with brushes and water pans.

Divide the class into committees to represent each of the old western trails. After research, each committee draws its trail with a different color, and decides on an appropriate scene, or scenes, to place along the route. Insist that all pictures be put away before the sketching begins. They should be consulted again only for final details, if necessary. Drawings can be done directly on the large map, but it is easier to have them done elsewhere, cut out, and pasted in place. See that any lettering is legible and even.

Dioramas of Early American Scenes

LEVEL 5

See
ACTIVITY 23

SUGGESTED MATERIALS: Shoe boxes, assorted construction paper, pipe-cleaners, paste, scissors, and odds and ends.

Ask each child to bring a shoe box or very small cardboard carton to class. Explain that a diorama is like a little stage with background scenery, props, and people. Have them recall typical early American scenes that they could use. Continue the list long enough to get away from the commonplace. Suggest that pipe-cleaners be used to form figures which can be dressed with scraps of construction paper. Encourage ingenuity in creating background, furniture, or whatever else is needed by showing enthusiasm as the dioramas develop.

Perils of Pioneer Life

LEVEL 5

See
ACTIVITIES 36,
38–40, and 42

SUGGESTED MATERIALS: $3' \times 4'$ background paper for a mural or Manila paper $12'' \times 18''$ for individual projects, and chalk, crayons, or tempera paint with brushes.

By stories and dramatization try to develop a real empathy among the children for the perils of pioneer life. Animals, Indians, unknown trails, weather phenomena, and lack of food, are a few of the possible problems. Try to persuade them to think of their illustrations in the first person (there I stood with a wild bear coming toward me), and to make the pictures big and vivid. For example, just the head of the bear, with his mouth wide open, might fill the page to portray the idea suggested above.

Papier-Mâché Project

LEVEL 6

SUGGESTED MATERIALS: Balloons of desired sizes, paper toweling, library paste, Plasticene, construction paper, and tempera paint with brushes.

Piñatas or native masks might be the inspiration for this project, depending on what area of the world the class has been studying. Bring many examples to the attention of the class so they will have a rich background from which to conceive their own original variations. For the Piñatas inflate balloons and cover their entire surface first with torn 1″ strips of toweling dipped in water and then, crisscrossed, with three more layers of strips dipped briefly in a thin paste solution (library paste diluted with water, or a mixture of flour and water). When the covering is dry, deflate the balloon and remove it. Paint gay designs on the Piñatas with tempera and add appendages of construction paper. For masks, model the foundation of Plasticene. Emphasize sunken eyes, protruding noses, and other features. Cover the Plasticene with torn toweling strips, as above, and when they are dry decorate the masks with paint and construction paper.

Painting with Brush

LEVEL 6

SUGGESTED MATERIALS: Manila or white drawing paper 9″ × 24″, black tempera paint, and pointed brushes.

Show the class many drawings done with brush strokes in black on white. Preferably choose some from a country they have studied. The oriental cultures have a vast treasury of such drawings, but they can also be found in Mexico (by Diego Rivera, for example) and elsewhere. Direct the students' attention to the simplicity with which these artists draw with the brush, achieving much of their effect with subtle changes in the width or darkness of their brush stroke. After the students have practiced with black paint and brush, challenge them to paint a simple picture without previously drawing it in pencil.

Native-Style Pottery

LEVEL 6

See
ACTIVITY 74

SUGGESTED MATERIALS: Water-base clay, a protected surface to work on (oilcloth is good), and modeling tools.

Bring many examples or photographs of the pottery typical of the culture the class is studying. Direct attention to special types and characteristics of the designs used in decoration. Discuss the ways in which craftsmen native to a culture develop variations on the prevalent themes. Show students how to build rings of firm, round coils onto a circular base of ½″ thick clay. With careful smoothing, all the indications of the coils should disappear. If a kiln is available, consider using underglaze for the design. Otherwise paint with tempera, and spray on clear plastic to protect the surface.

Contributions to Mankind

LEVEL 6

See
ACTIVITY 72

SUGGESTED MATERIALS: Battleship linoleum or potatoes, cutters or knives, water-soluble printers' ink or thick tempera paint, plain or colored newsprint 9″ × 12″, heavier paper for booklet covers, and paper fasteners. A brayer may be used to roll on printer's ink.

After an intensive study of a culture, hold a class discussion of the major contributions of that civilization to mankind. If the list is long enough, have each member of the class symbolize an achievement in a design cut into linoleum or a cross section of a potato. The number of prints should be sufficient to give each member of the class one copy to assemble into his booklet. When the list is quite brief, the class can be divided into committees within which the designing, cutting, printing, and written description can be assigned. Assemble the newsprint pages within covers of heavier paper.

Mural-Map of World Resources

LEVEL 7

See
ACTIVITY 68

SUGGESTED MATERIALS: Background paper about 3′ × 5′, an opaque projector, stencil paper or light cardboard, sharp blades for cutting cardboard, tempera paint, and stiff brushes.

Use a projector to outline a map of the world on background paper. During the class discussion list resources valuable to man. If there are more items on the list than class members, establish priorities. Have each student choose one resource and make a simple design symbol for it. Demonstrate the need for cutting clear, sharp lines in cardboard or stencil paper. Show how to wipe excess paint off a brush, and, holding it vertically, lightly daub paint onto open spaces in the stencil. After careful research, allow each student to stencil his symbol onto the map at the places where his resources are found. Reserve an area for a legible key to the symbols.

Display Panels

LEVEL 7

See
ACTIVITY 22

SUGGESTED MATERIALS: Plywood panels 4' × 8', planks 1" × 8" × 4' for each plywood panel, paper to cover, a crosscut saw, construction paper, scissors, and paste.

Plan with the class an effective location to display art work for a special occasion. Borrow or purchase several plywood panels. Have students cut two "feet" from the plank for each panel. These pieces should be shaped like a pyramid, about 2' along the base, and with a groove cut down 4" from the apex to admit the width of the plywood. If covering paper is fastened carefully, the panels can be returned unharmed when the display is over. Discuss the layout for the display as a design problem with the students making suggestions. Letters may be cut from construction paper for eye-catching phrases.

Geographical Features

LEVEL 7

See
ACTIVITIES
11 *and* 43

SUGGESTED MATERIALS: 12" × 18" drawing paper, newspapers, paste, assorted natural material, wood 2' × 3' if the project is to be three-dimensional.

Review with the class the meaning of the terms used to describe geographic features. Challenge them to draw a plan of an island which will incorporate within its bounds as many of these features as there are room for—peninsulas, bays, rivers, volcanos, lakes, etc. If the interest is intense, continue the project by having students construct a model of one or more plans using improvisations of natural materials on a papier-mâché pulp base. These might later be loaned to lower grades to help them understand geographical terms.

Stained-Glass Windows

LEVEL 7

SUGGESTED MATERIALS: Manila paper cut to the size of the classroom window panes, wax crayons, linseed or cooking oil (1 cup), turpentine (¼ cup), and broad brushes.

Consider whether to correlate this activity with the study of foreign cathedrals or Christmas. In either case, have numerous examples of stained-glass windows on hand, particularly those with the simplicity and limited colors of the medieval period. Show the class how the bold black division lines create unity and make the colors more brilliant. Emphasize the need for thoroughly covering the papers with wax crayon. When the student has completed the design, he should brush the oil-and-turpentine mixture onto the back of the design to create translucency and fasten the design to a window with transparent tape.

Historical Movie

LEVEL 8

See
ACTIVITY 47

SUGGESTED MATERIALS: Two broom poles or a more elaborate box device with a pole that turns on either side, Manila paper the correct width to fit rollers, masking tape, and crayons or paints with brushes.

Explain that these movies are simply a series of pictures unrolled in sequence between two rollers. Narration is presented to clarify the story. Once the principle is understood, some boys will probably volunteer to make a more elaborate device, but this is not necessary. Emphasize the need for careful planning and research by committees. Before beginning their drawings for movies, students should put away all reference material. They can check the details later, away from the working area. A committee should be formed to tape together the drawings and fasten them to the poles.

"Then" and "Now" Booklet

LEVEL **8**

SUGGESTED MATERIALS: Newsprint 12″ × 18″ (to be folded for interior pages), construction paper 12″ × 18″, and paper fasteners.

With the class discuss the contrasts between everyday objects used in pioneer days and those of today. List them on the chalkboard. Explain that drawing for historical accuracy requires significant detail, but that there is no need to worry about exact proportions. In other words, the procedure is to look hard at the object, or a picture of it, turn away, and quickly draw without erasing. "Then" and "Now" could be on the same or facing pages. Challenge students to do all their pages without erasures, then to make only the absolute minimum of changes to clarify the communication. This activity makes students more perceptive. Accept all products.

Time Lines of United States History

LEVEL **8**

See
ACTIVITY 48

SUGGESTED MATERIALS: Drawing paper 12″ × 36″ or larger and a choice of the media available.

Explain that a time line is made up of a sequence of related events. Challenge the pupils to review their study of United States history and to think of possible subjects for time lines—such as changes in communication, transportation, or clothing, perhaps. Usually five drawings is the minimum for a meaningful sequence, with each picture dated. Divide the class into committees each to produce one time line. Remind the students that reference material should not be visible while drawings are being worked on. Allow them freedom in their choice of media.

Contemporary Cartoons

LEVEL **8**

SUGGESTED MATERIALS: White drawing paper 9″ × 12″ and pens and ink or felt-tip pens.

Gather significant examples of historical cartoons on various subjects. Define limitations that students should consider in deciding on an idea for their cartoons. Emphasize that originality and thought have always been valued more highly than the quality of the drawing. Some of the best cartoonists have not been realistic in their drawings. Encourage drawing directly with pen and ink, or a felt-tip pen. A complete redrawing is, in most cases, preferable to a much-erased product. Evaluate the communication of ideas, not drawing accuracy.

SECTION FIVE

Using Animals in Elementary-School Art

OBJECTIVES

To sharpen the perception of characteristics that differentiate various animals.
To create an awareness of a wide variety of animals and their common qualities.
To help children identify animals with the animals' usual environments.

All the art activities in this section should be preceded by extensive observation and discussion aimed at developing the child's ability to generalize, to observe relationships, and to perceive differences. Real animals should be used whenever possible. Three-dimensional models are helpful if there are a number available. Photographs can be used successfully if there are enough of them to show many views of an animal. It is very important that the animal pictures, if they are used, be out of sight during the time the children are working. An occasional supplementary glance might be allowed, away from the working area, for older students who are concerned with accurate details.

Once the children have achieved a vivid awareness of the animal, they should feel free to interpret and express the subject each in his own way. NO CRITICIZING SHOULD BE DONE ONCE THE CHILDREN START THEIR WORK. Some will have absorbed more than others. Research studies show that perception is a highly individualized matter, but that it can be sharpened. Motivation and directed observation make the difference and provide a rich reservoir of material for creative art. Fear of failure, however, stifles creativity, so children must be allowed to interpret in their own way the facts they have gathered. The teacher's enthusiastic praise and acceptance of their work will be reflected in their spontaneity and originality.

Animals should not be used as art activities unless the class is interested in them.

Pets

LEVEL I

SUGGESTED MATERIALS: Newsprint 18″ × 24″, tempera paint with brushes, and primary wax crayons.

If possible visit a pet store with the class. Focus attention on special features of the various animals observed. Ask each child to decide which animal he would like for a pet. If facilities or supplies are limited, have the children "draw" their pictures with black tempera, using a stiff-bristled brush. Big primary crayons can be used later for color. Emphasize making the pets as large as possible on the paper. In any empty spaces suggest adding grass or things the animals might like to play with.

Animals in the Grass

LEVEL I

SUGGESTED MATERIALS: 12″ × 18″ light blue paper, assorted colored paper including greens, scissors, and paste.

After the basic supplies have been distributed, spend about three minutes telling the class a highly dramatic story leading up to the line, "And then I saw an animal hiding in the grass." Ask the children to provide the ending by cutting the animal out of colored paper and pasting it, plus much tall grass, on the light blue paper. Treat their questions gaily, implying that the beast was most unusual looking. Show enthusiasm for imaginative results.

Cats

LEVEL 1

See
ACTIVITY 52

SUGGESTED MATERIALS: Manila or rougher paper 12″ × 18″ and chalk or small pieces of wax crayon.

During a visit with a cat, direct the children's attention to its little ears, long tail, and whiskers. Later, as supplies are distributed, help them to recall these catlike features. Ask the children if they can make their cat big enough so his little ears touch the top edge of the paper and his little rounded paws touch the bottom edge. If they are using crayons, encourage them to use the side of the crayon for soft, furry edges.

Elephants

LEVEL 1

See
ACTIVITY 57

SUGGESTED MATERIALS: Gray construction paper, bright-colored paper scraps, paste, and scissors.

Unless there is a circus or a zoo nearby, bring in many pictures of elephants for the class to examine. Some children might be able to bring small carvings of the animals. Direct their observation to the big, curving trunk up front and the little tail in the back, with a big, hill-like hump in between. Note the bulky legs and fan-shaped ears. Give the children gray paper and scissors. After they cut out the elephants, let them choose colored scraps to paste on for saddles or other decorations. A parade of elephants across the top of the chalkboard is fun. Use bright-colored paper for a background.

Cows

LEVEL 2

See
ACTIVITY 56

SUGGESTED MATERIALS: Manila or light blue paper 12″ × 18″ and assorted tempera paint, with brushes or wax crayons.

Visit real cows or bring many pictures of cows to class. Direct the attention of the children to the relative flatness of the back. Ask them if cows have soft, rounded curves, as do cats. Have them notice the small size of the head compared to the bulk of the rest of the animal, and the tail. Challenge the children to create a large herd of cows. Encourage them to add grass for the cows to eat, trees to shelter them, and perhaps a pond for them to drink from.

Rabbits

LEVEL 2

See
ACTIVITY 51

SUGGESTED MATERIALS: Light blue paper 12″ × 18″ and chalk of several colors, including white.

Usually a rabbit is available for observation. If not, use numerous pictures. Direct the children's attention to the bent rear legs of the rabbit, an aid to hopping. Ask them whether the rabbit's head resembles a cat's. A rabbit's tail and ears make him an easy animal to identify and draw. Encourage children to draw whole families of rabbits with white chalk, sitting and jumping in grass and flowers.

Tigers

LEVEL 2

See
ACTIVITY 52

SUGGESTED MATERIALS: Manila paper 12″ × 18″ and assorted chalk, wax crayons, or tempera paint with brushes.

Review the distinguishing features of the cat family learned on level 1. Unless there is a local zoo, depend on many pictures of tigers to help the class compare them in appearance to domestic cats. The stripes will undoubtedly impress the children, but the more observant will notice other distinguishing characteristics, too. The art expression could be in any of the above media, or in cut paper. Ask them to show whether they prefer their tigers in cages or in their native habitat.

Birds

LEVEL 2

See
ACTIVITY 54

SUGGESTED MATERIALS: Assorted large scraps of colored construction paper, scissors, and paste.

From time to time, call the children's attention to birds within their view. Have bird books on the library table. One day ask the children to help make a list of characteristics that differentiate birds from other forms of animal life. They will probably mention beaks and wings first. Give them access to large scraps of colored paper. Encourage them to create birds, real or imaginary. Have a large tree of cut paper for their birds to perch on or suspend them from a large, leafless branch of a real tree. Enjoy them with the children.

Dogs

LEVEL 3

See
ACTIVITY 50

SUGGESTED MATERIALS: Newsprint 18″ × 24″ and assorted tempera paint with brushes.

Dogs are so common that many children have not looked at one carefully. Ask them to observe how dogs differ from cats. Most children will see the obvious differences. A few will become aware of subtleties such as leg conformation. Once the children are intensely aware of what makes a dog look doglike, they can use the animal freely in their art expression. Encourage such titles as "My dog and I had an adventure" or "I would like to have this dog for a friend."

Camels

LEVEL 3

SUGGESTED MATERIALS depend on the class decision.

The need for a clear concept of the appearance of a camel is often strongest around Christmas. Collect pictures showing the animal. Encourage the children to bring them in also. After observing many views, help them to make some generalizations. Is the neck longer than the legs? Is the nose like that of a dog? What kind of a tail does a camel have? Which is more suitable to the present need: a camel with one hump or two? The art expression that results depends on the class's plans.

Snakes

LEVEL 3

SUGGESTED MATERIALS; Construction paper in assorted colors, scissors, and paste.

If harmless snakes are available, let the children view them. Direct questions to sharpen their perception of the shape of the head and of the eyes. Where is the snake the widest? Does it taper off gradually or not at all? Show them many pictures of snakes with beautiful designs on their backs. Suggest that they cut snakes out of the colored paper and paste designs on their backs. A fringe of green paper along an edge of a bulletin board would give the finished snakes a place to hide.

Chickens

LEVEL 3

SUGGESTED MATERIALS: Green construction paper 12″ × 18″ and assorted chalks.

If there are live chickens nearby, let the children study them. Make the children aware of the small size of the head in relation to the body. Have them trace in the air the long curve from the neck down and up to the tail. Focus their attention on details such as the number and direction of the tail feathers and the shape of the eyes. Some children will be impressed with one detail, others with another. Suggest that they make a whole flock of chickens on the green paper, adding grass for them to hide their eggs in and perhaps chicken houses.

Butterflies

LEVEL 4

SUGGESTED MATERIALS: Manila paper 9″ × 12″, assorted wax crayons, a mixture of 3 parts linseed or salad oil to one part turpentine, and brushes.

Collect real butterflies or many pictures of them. Help the children generalize on the shape of the body and the antennas. Guide them in comparing the wing types, and in enjoying the marvelous colors and designs. Later ask them to create their own special butterflies. Encourage them to distribute the rich color of the wax crayons evenly. Show them how coating the backs of the papers with the oil solution makes them translucent. Perhaps they can be placed on the windows for everyone to enjoy.

Sheep

LEVEL 4

SUGGESTED MATERIALS: There are many possibilities—chalk, cotton, sponges with tempera paint, or cut paper on other appropriate paper.

As children observe real or pictured sheep, help them to discover that the real shape is determined by the wool coat. Have them notice the distinctive contour of the ears and nose. Unless the class has a particular project in mind for which sheep are needed, have them experiment with various materials to see which best depicts the fuzziness of the sheep's outline. The culmination might be an outdoor pasture scene.

Horses

LEVEL 4

See
ACTIVITY 53

SUGGESTED MATERIALS: Manila paper 12″ × 18″ and crayons or tempera paint with brushes.

Live horses can be found for observation in almost any locale. Call the children's attention to the long neck and nose, the shape of the head, and the set of the ears. So many children's drawings of horses resemble dogs that later in the classroom the children might compare the appearance of the two animals to sharpen their perception of the differences. Horses can be related to many scenes, such as ranches, races, and farms, for art expression.

Members of the Cat Family

See
ACTIVITY 52

LEVEL 4

SUGGESTED MATERIALS: Manila paper 12″ × 18″ and felt-tip pens, if available, or assorted chalks.

Unless there is a zoo close by, use pictures of cats, tigers, lions, and other members of the cat family to discover what features they have in common and how they differ. Discuss with the children the lithe, graceful movements of the animals. From the head to the tail is a long series of undulating curves. The art expression that grows out of this investigation might place the "cats" in their native habitat, the circus, or the zoo.

Animals in Motion

LEVEL 5

SUGGESTED MATERIALS: Manila paper 12″ × 18″, background paper 3′ × 5′, and crayons or assorted tempera paint with brushes.

Animals are commonly drawn by young children as stationary, often with just two legs. Some children on this level, however, will be ready to observe how an animal's legs look when they are moving. Extensive observation of the animals found in the vicinity is useful. Bring in pictures for this purpose if excursions are not possible. For those children who enjoy details, discuss the numerous joints in the animal's legs, and which way they bend. Help children to see that on a flat surface, such as a paper, the animal's legs that are farther away will be shorter. Allow them to use as much of this information as they have absorbed in their art expression. The idea of a "Peaceable Kingdom," where the lion and the lamb play together, would make an interesting mural or individual picture.

Oxen and Similar Animals

See
ACTIVITY 56

LEVEL 5

SUGGESTED MATERIALS: Background paper 3′ × 5′ and a choice of the available media.

Collect pictures of oxen, cows, and other cattle for the purpose of having the class compare the characteristic features of each with the others. This will sharpen their perception and give them confidence to use these animals in, for example, a wagon-train mural. Direct the children's attention first of all to the over-all form of the body, next to the relative size and characteristic shape of the various parts, and last of all to special details, such as the set of the ears and the tail. The choice of media from those available might be made by the children.

Mice

LEVEL 5

SUGGESTED MATERIALS: Gray or white paper 12″ × 18″ and assorted colored chalks.

Children usually enjoy having mice around for observation. However, if mice are not available, bring in some good pictures of them. Guide the children to perceive the over-all shape of the mice. Enjoy with the class their inquisitive, pointed, little noses. Challenge the children to create a scene that includes a family of mice doing something interesting. Encourage them to include sufficient background to identify where the mice are living.

All Kinds of Dogs

LEVEL 5

See
ACTIVITY 50

SUGGESTED MATERIALS: Large 18″ × 24″ drawing paper with tempera paint and brushes, or 12″ × 18″ Manila paper and crayons.

Arrange for a few of the children to bring in their dogs, if possible, or, if not, pictures of them. Add to the collection enough pictures to show a wide variety of shapes, sizes, and colors. Review the typical dog characteristics discovered on level 3. The study might culminate in large pictures of single dogs, or scenes that include several dogs. In either case, emphasize the personality rather than the breed of the dogs.

Pond Creatures

LEVEL 6

See
ACTIVITY 38

SUGGESTED MATERIALS: Drawing paper 12″ × 18″ and water colors with brushes and water pans or assorted wax crayons.

This activity should be done at the same time as, or after, the natural environment exploration of the appearance of water surfaces (section six, level 6). Through pictures or observation at a nearby pond, give the children an opportunity to observe and compare swans and ducks. Ask them, "Which one has the longest neck?" and, "How do their bills differ?" After other questions have sharpened their perception, have the children plan pond scenes which include both birds. Crayon resist is a good technique to use if white wax crayons are available.

Monkeys Are Active

LEVEL 6

See
ACTIVITY 58

SUGGESTED MATERIALS: Manila paper 12″ × 18″ and assorted wax crayons, including broken brown crayons.

A nearby zoo, or many pictures of monkeys, should be used to study the features of the animals. Help the children notice characteristic details in the size and placement of the ears, and the shape of the head. Show them briefly that one of the easiest ways to draw monkeys in action, is with the side of a short piece of brown crayon. The arms and legs can be defined in a few strokes. Perhaps this activity can be incorporated in the "jungle" suggested for this level in section six, level 6.

Reindeer

LEVEL 6

SUGGESTED MATERIALS: A choice of paper and available media.

Help the children compare the shape of the reindeer to that of a horse. Ask such questions as, "How do they differ?" "Are the tails the same?" "Do the antlers grow from the top or side of the head?" and, "Is the neck longer or shorter?" The setting in which the animals are drawn would depend on the time of the year or the units being studied.

Jungle Animals

LEVEL 6

SUGGESTED MATERIALS: Assorted heavy construction paper or light cardboard, scissors, and paste.

Review with the class the jungle animals they have used in their art expression. Help the children plan a three-dimensional jungle. Stand-up animals can be made easily by cutting

U-shaped pieces of rather stiff paper or cardboard which, turned upside down, form the four legs of the beast. Vertical slits should be cut at the top of each set of legs to accommodate the body of the animal, which should have two short slits cut where the legs should be. The neck, head, body, and tail are made in one unit. Suggest that the characteristic feature of each animal should be emphasized. Improvising the jungle growth with construction paper will challenge a committee of students.

Wild Birds

LEVEL 7

See
ACTIVITY 54

SUGGESTED MATERIALS: Manila paper 12″ × 18″, assorted chalk or India ink and pen, water colors, and brushes.

Take the class on a bird walk if this can possibly be arranged. A feeding platform outside the classroom window would also help the students observe wild birds carefully. Challenge the class to develop their perception of the form of these birds. The size of the head in relation to the body, the shape of the beak, the angle of the tail feathers, as well as the coloring, can be studied. If possible, let the students choose between free interpretation of birds and foliage in chalk, or a more precise expression with India ink and water-color wash. In either case, allow the children to be selective rather than realistic.

Bears

LEVEL 7

SUGGESTED MATERIALS: Manila paper 12″ × 18″, assorted tempera paint, and stiff brushes or sponges.

Show the class many pictures of bears. Have them notice the shapes of their heads, noses, and ears. The appearance of the bear's legs in upright position, as well as when walking on all fours, will interest some students. Suggest that tempera paint used with a dry brush or a sponge will create the impression of fuzzy bulkiness typical of bears. Woods and a nearby cave entrance might complete the scene.

Deep-Sea Fish

LEVEL 7

See
ACTIVITY 55

SUGGESTED MATERIALS: Manila paper 12″ × 18″, assorted wax crayons, water colors, and brushes.

Discuss with the class the features common to most fish: head, eyes, mouth, tail, fins, and possibly scales. Have the students describe the innumerable possibilities for individual variations among species in length, color, etc. Remind them that no one has ever identified all the fish that might exist deep under the sea, so they can feel free to invent species. Challenge the students to create an imaginary underwater scene with fish of various sizes and shapes in bright-colored crayon. Seaweed, shells, and even treasure chests and ship wrecks can add interest. Later the scenes can be brushed over with a thin, watery, blue-green hue.

Prehistoric Animals

LEVEL 7

See
ACTIVITY 43

SUGGESTED MATERIALS: Old newspaper shredded into a cooking pot, wheat flour or library paste, paint, brushes, and old coat hangers.

Guide the class in an investigation of the various prehistoric animals. Some students may be able to bring to class the rubber models widely sold. Their reptilian characteristics or their resemblance to present-day animals can be discussed. Emphasize the special features such as the long necks and small heads of the dinosaur. Modeling prehistoric animals with cooked paper-pulp on a coat hanger wire framework might be the culmination of this activity. Since they are not supposed to be authentic, encourage gay decorative effects when the animals are painted.

Caged Birds

LEVEL 8

See
ACTIVITY 54

SUGGESTED MATERIALS: Colored construction paper 12″ × 18″, a variety of colored poster paper or other thin paper, paste, and scissors.

Bring a caged bird or two to class for a preparatory period of observation. Ask the students to note, in their visits to local stores, the amazing variety in decorative cages for birds. Guide a discussion of the various birds commonly kept as pets. Suggest the students cut the general shape of their chosen bird from colored paper and then add details such as beak and eyes. Let them have fun designing a fantastic cage for their birds from cut paper. They can paste everything against a background color that lends gay contrast to the picture.

Eagle Designs

LEVEL 8

SUGGESTED MATERIALS: White drawing paper 9″ × 12″, colored inks or assorted tempera paint, pens or brushes, and perhaps plaster of Paris in a box lid.

Direct the class in an investigation of the eagle as used in designs from the Colonial Period to the present. The class will discover that certain characteristics, such as the talons and the curved beak, identify the bird. Suggest that they feature an eagle in a design of their own. Help them think of the feathers as a line design, and the colors they use as decorative. Instead of a drawing, the eagle design could be carved in plaster of Paris that has been poured into a reinforced box lid. Simple paring knives can be used as carving tools.

Wolves

LEVEL 8

See
ACTIVITIES
41 *and* 50

SUGGESTED MATERIALS: White drawing or charcoal paper 12″ × 18″, charcoal, and chamois or paper tissues for blending.

Show pictures that will enable the class to compare wolves and dogs. They have many characteristics in common, but perceptive students will be able to identify the source of the "wolfish" look. Consider, with the class, the threat of wolf packs to the pioneers. Have them draw the animals in a wilderness setting. Emphasize the strong contrasts between rich blacks, pale grays, and the white of the paper, which are found in good charcoal drawings.

Sketching Pets

LEVEL 8

See
ACTIVITIES
50 *and* 52

SUGGESTED MATERIALS: Drawing paper 9″ × 12″ and soft lead pencil, charcoal, or wax crayons.

Encourage students to make quick sketches of pets or animals in their neighborhood. Emphasize the importance of looking at the animal first until the over-all shape is firmly perceived. Convince them that if they start with a light sketch of the larger form, then the relationships of the parts such as the head, the legs, and the smaller details will be evident. If an animal can be persuaded to pose for a few minutes in the classroom, this could be the culmination of the previous experiences.

SECTION SIX

Using the Natural Environment in Elementary-School Art

OBJECTIVES

To provide the children with some technical means that simplify the problems of including a variety of natural objects in art expression.

To encourage children to use many variations of one natural form by stimulating their awareness of these differences.

To sharpen children's perceptions of their natural environment by close observation and group discussion of what they have observed.

These activities involving our natural environment should be preceded by considerable observation of the subject matter to be used. Some children will never notice the beauties with which they are surrounded unless they are made aware of them by a perceptive teacher. Once the class discussion is concluded, each child should feel free to interpret in his own way what he has seen. CRITICISM CAN BE HARMFUL WHEN IT INTERFERES WITH THE CHILD'S OWN WAY OF SEEING THINGS.

Grow a Garden

LEVEL I

See
ACTIVITY 61

SUGGESTED MATERIALS: Newsprint 18″ × 24″, black tempera paint, brushes, and wax crayons or assorted tempera paint.

If possible, take the class to enjoy a neighborhood flower garden. If not, substitute many pictures of garden flowers. By questions, bring to the children's attention the diversity of flowers and leaves. Tell them that they are going to have the fun of filling every bit of their paper with flowers and leaves. For a first painting experience, or with limited facilities, the children can paint the outlines and then color in later with large crayons. Emphasize filling every empty space.

Grass Can Be Many Kinds of Green

LEVEL I

See
ACTIVITY 39

SUGGESTED MATERIALS: Newsprint 18″ × 24″ with assorted tempera paint and brushes, or 12″ × 18″ Manila paper and assorted crayons, including at least three varieties of green.

Walk to some area nearby where the children can observe a variety of greens in the trees, shrubbery, and grass. If this is impossible, substitute pictures showing yellow-greens, blue-greens, dark greens, and light greens. Help them to enjoy this variety within a color. Let the class observe while yellow and blue are added to separate jars of basic green. Add black and white to two other jars. If the class is going to use crayons, show them the range they can achieve. Encourage them to blend yellow and blue over the other greens. Challenge them to see how many different greens they can include in their out-of-doors picture. Ask them what action they are planning on the grass for emphasis.

Trees Are Widest at the Bottom

LEVEL 1

See
Activity 64

SUGGESTED MATERIALS: Light blue paper 12″ × 18″ and tempera paint with brushes or assorted wax crayons.

Direct children's observation on several occasions to trees in the vicinity. By questions, bring them to observe that tree trunks are widest where they leave the ground, then get smaller and smaller until near the top, and far out on all sides, are many tiny twigs. Encourage the children to "grow" their trees from the ground up, using the side of a wax crayon or brush and paint. Definitely discourage the use of pencils first. Show delight over drawings with prolific twigs and branches. Ask them what they can have up in their tree for emphasis.

Skies Come Down to Where the Ground Begins

LEVEL 1

See
Activities
26 *and* 66

SUGGESTED MATERIALS: Newsprint 18″ × 24″ and assorted tempera paint with brushes, or 12″ × 18″ Manila paper and crayons.

Have the children observe how the sky goes down between the houses or touches the nearby mountains or plains. Do this on numerous occasions before mentioning it during art class. Plan one day, perhaps several months after the lesson spent on trees, to have the children paint or crayon their sky and ground in first to completely cover the paper. Then, after a review of the way trees grow, challenge them to see how many trees they can place in their pictures. This activity could be planned for two days if the class tires easily.

Trees Grow Many Branches

LEVEL 2

See
Activity 64

SUGGESTED MATERIALS: Newsprint 18″ × 24″ and assorted tempera paint with brushes, or 12″ × 18″ Manila paper and crayons.

Review with the class the concept of tree trunks being widest at their base, and gradually growing smaller and smaller branches in the upper portions. Have the class try to count the number of twigs on a nearby tree. Later suggest that they make a picture using trees with many branches and twigs. If the class is unresponsive or lacking in enthusiasm, challenge them to see who can place the most twigs and branches on one tree. Suggest adding foliage if there is time.

The Sky Is Always Changing

LEVEL 2

See
Activity 26

SUGGESTED MATERIALS: Newsprint 12″ × 18″ and either tempera paint with small mixing pans and brushes or small pieces of assorted crayons.

Over a period of time call to the attention of the class how the sky is constantly changing in color and cloud formations. Encourage the children to notice unusual sky effects. One day give each child several sheets of newsprint and ask him to experiment to see what beautiful skies he can make. Show appreciation of lovely colors or unusual clouds. If there is time, suggest that each child select his favorite sky and make something in front of it that denotes action. Birds, airplanes, and spacecraft, are some of the things the children will think of.

Many Trees in a Forest

LEVEL 2

See
ACTIVITY 62

SUGGESTED MATERIALS: Paper approximately 3′ × 5′, tempera paint, brushes, and small pieces of sponge.

Recall the happy experiences the children have had making beautiful skies and trees with many twigs. Show them the paper and explain that it is big enough for a whole forest of trees. After a committee paints a beautiful sky and some ground for the trees to grow from, let each child take a turn adding his tree to the forest. This can continue over several days. If there are seasonal changes, such as spring blossoms or autumn color outdoors, they might be added later with a sponge. Children might suggest other additions if their interest holds. Little animals can appear in the forest.

Mountains Are All Shapes and Sizes

LEVEL 2

See
ACTIVITY 67

SUGGESTED MATERIALS: Manila paper 12″ × 18″, assorted crayons or chalk, and fine sandpaper.

If there are nearby mountains, direct the class's attention to their shapes. Have them trace the tops with their fingers. Direct their observation to the smaller foothills. Later, inside, challenge them to fill a paper with mountains and hills using the sides of their crayons or chalk. Praise variety in size, shape, and color. This activity is particularly fascinating to children if they use wax crayons on fine sandpaper, and then either place their pictures in a 200° oven or in the sun until the crayon melts.

Trees Have Many Different Shapes

LEVEL 3

See
ACTIVITY 64

SUGGESTED MATERIALS: Light blue paper 12″ × 18″, assorted pieces of colored paper, scissors, and paste.

Use actual observation or many pictures to make the children aware of the variations in the shapes of trees. Have children take turns describing different trees they have seen, perhaps painting the shape with clear water on the chalkboard. Let the children see how many shapes they can cut from different shades of green paper, adding trunks and branches of darker colors. For special interest, suggest they partly hide something cut out of colored paper behind one or more of the trees. Animals, people, or Hansel and Gretel's candy house are possibilities.

Flower Varieties

LEVEL 3

See
ACTIVITY 7

SUGGESTED MATERIALS: Manila paper 9″ × 12″, assorted wax crayons, and small metal "tools" such as nail files, bobby pins, or large carpenters' nails.

Encourage the children to collect flowers and flower pictures in order to enjoy the infinite variations of flowers in size, color, shape, and petal detail. Review the technique for making crayon etchings. Have them cover their papers with many-sized circles of bright-colored crayon, and the remaining paper with yellow, yellow-green, or another light color. After covering the page completely with black crayon, the children will find they can still locate most of their circles to turn them into flowers with all varieties of petals and textures. Encourage them to scrape away areas as well as lines.

Rain Changes the Look of Things

LEVEL 3

See
ACTIVITIES 38
and 59

SUGGESTED MATERIALS: Manila paper 12″ × 18″, wax crayons, a small quantity of black tempera paint in water, and a brush.

Direct the children's observation to changes that occur outdoors on rainy days. If possible, do this activity where the children can continue to observe the rain and its effects on people and nature—the trees, the sky, etc. Suggest crayon for the basic drawing, to be washed over later with the watery gray tempera paint. Before the children apply the wash, have them examine their pictures to see if they have some bright areas of emphasis that will add interest and variety, such as colorful rain clothes brightening a street scene.

Variations in Ground Color

LEVEL 3

See
ACTIVITY 39

SUGGESTED MATERIALS: Manila paper 12″ × 18″ and assorted crayons and chalks.

Encourage the children to collect many dirt samples in small glass jars to observe the color range from yellowish sand to reddish clay. If this variety is not available locally, use pictures that emphasize ground color. Show the children how blending one hue on top of another produces variations. Discuss surface variations created by the plow making long furrows, or wagons cutting ruts in the dirt. While the children are creating the ground and the sky, start them thinking about putting something into the picture for emphasis and interest.

Fruit Trees

LEVEL 4

See
ACTIVITY 64

SUGGESTED MATERIALS: Light blue paper 12″ × 18″, with assorted crayons, or water colors, or tempera paint with brush, on white paper 12″ × 18″.

Review the concepts of trees developed on previous levels. Take the class to observe a tree loaded with fruit, or show many pictures on the subject. Discourage any preliminary drawing in pencil. If the children are painting, discuss unusual sky and ground colors. Let them paint the background first, and then, when it is dry, they can paint the trees directly on top of it. Have them view their pictures from a distance to make certain the fruit is clearly visible. Some children may want to add people picking the fruit.

"Rainy" Water Colors

LEVEL 4

See
ACTIVITY 59

SUGGESTED MATERIALS: White paper 12″ × 18″, water colors, and brushes.

Gather pictures—water colors, if possible—that show rainy, stormy skies. Choose a wet day to start this project, suggesting that children note the sky and cloud colors out-of-doors. Tell them not to worry if their colors run into each other, since this blurry effect is characteristic of rain. Emphasize that they should create something in the foreground that is bright or very dark for emphasis, before they call the picture finished.

Windy Weather

LEVEL 4

SUGGESTED MATERIALS: Manila paper 12″ × 18″ and assorted chalk.

See
ACTIVITY 60

A windy hour on the playground is good preparation for this activity. Ask the children to recall the look of things in the wind. Make a list of specific items such as kites blowing about, trees leaning over, and grass bending in one direction. Ask the class how people react to wind. Encourage them to cover the paper completely with their chalks, not forgetting to create a center of interest for emphasis—perhaps people being blown along by the wind.

Favorite Flowers

LEVEL 4

See
ACTIVITY 61

SUGGESTED MATERIALS: Black paper 12″ × 18″ and assorted chalk.

If it is feasible, have each child bring one flower, his favorite kind, to class. Have each child examine his flower very closely, and then, bit by bit, slowly pull it apart to see how marvelously it is put together. Put the remnants in a wastebasket, out of sight, and ask the children to re-create their flower, bigger than life, on their paper. Challenge them to make it almost as wide across as their paper. Encourage them to add leaves if they have space left over.

Varieties of Palm Trees

LEVEL 5

See
ACTIVITY 24

SUGGESTED MATERIALS: Light blue or yellow paper 12″ × 18″, assorted colored paper including several shades of green, paste, and scissors.

If the children do not live in a warm climate, show them pictures of many varieties of palm trees, from the very tall, straight type to the gracefully bending coconut palm and the short, lush, date palm. Help them to discover the long, banana-shaped individual leaves that are characteristic of the tree. They will find it great fun to cut the leaves from the various shades of green paper and to assemble them on trunks cut from other paper. The picture can be of a tropical island, Hawaiian Park, Florida Beach, or California Plaza with flowers and other details for interest.

Deep Forests

LEVEL 5

See
ACTIVITY 62

SUGGESTED MATERIALS: Manila or other drawing paper 12″ × 18″, tempera or water-color paint, and brushes.

Visit a nearby woods or exhibit many pictures of deep forests to help the children become aware of the vast number of overlapping trees in such a scene. Appeal to their imagination by helping them visualize Indians or pioneers penetrating dense forests. Let them recall earlier experiences with trees on previous levels. Encourage them to paint trunks and foliage directly without prior pencil-sketching. Remind them that they can do a great deal of overlapping and allow small trees to grow between big trees. Grass, shrubbery, and flowers might be added, if needed, for emphasis in the foreground. Perhaps some children will choose to place Indians or pioneers in the scene.

Making Nature Look Solid

LEVEL 5

See
ACTIVITY 39

SUGGESTED MATERIALS: Manila paper 12″ × 18″ and assorted crayons.

On a sunny day take the class outside—to a park, if possible—where they can take time to look around them. Direct their attention to the dark and light sides of tree trunks. Help them to see form created by dark and light in the foliage of the trees and bushes. Later, in their classroom, guide the children to discover how they can create an appearance of solidity in things by making one side dark and graduating the color to very light on the opposite side. Have them experiment with tree trunks on one side of their paper and then turn the paper over and create an outdoor scene applying what they have learned.

Three-Dimensional Flowers

LEVEL 5

See
ACTIVITY 19

SUGGESTED MATERIALS: Colored construction paper, scissors, paste, and material for stems, such as pipe-cleaners, thin wooden skewers, or soda straws.

On an early spring day suggest to the class that it might be fun to get a head start on spring by creating gay make-believe flowers on stems. Show them how to roll petals over a pencil to make them curl. Have them start on the flowers while they are considering the problem of what to use for stems. Praise unusual ideas as you observe them, to encourage originality in color combinations and form. Place flowers on chosen stems and then in containers.

Jungles Are Crowded

LEVEL 6

See
ACTIVITY 38

SUGGESTED MATERIALS: Manila paper 12″ × 18″, assorted crayons, water-color paint, and brushes.

Review with the class their innumerable previous experiences with trees, flowers, and forests. Introduce the concept of jungles as being practically impenetrable tangles crowded with trees, bushes, flowers, and many kinds of living creatures. Encourage them, taking odd moments, on several days, until they each have completely filled their papers. Remind them that the light in the jungle is somewhat dimmed by all the vegetation. They can achieve this effect by washing grayish-green water color over the entire paper.

Sunsets Are Colorful

LEVEL 6

See
ACTIVITY 66

SUGGESTED MATERIALS: Manila paper 12″ × 18″, assorted tempera paint, inch-square sponges, and possibly black paper 12″ × 18″.

Recall, by class discussion, the beautiful sunsets the children have seen. Emphasize the flaming mixtures of color. Suggest that they can achieve these effects by dipping the sponge in the paint lightly, squeezing it slightly, and then daubing their paper. The application of one hue on the other is fascinating to children. They might enjoy creating the silhouette of buildings in a city, or some other scene, from the black paper to place against the sky.

Water Can Be Painted Many Ways

LEVEL 6

See
ACTIVITY 63

SUGGESTED MATERIALS: White drawing paper 12″ × 18″, water-color paint, and brushes.

If possible, spend some time as a class observing the surface of a nearby body of water. Have the children collect photographs and paintings showing the surface of water. Pass them around for the purpose of discerning the variations in surface texture, color, and value that can create a watery effect. Put the reference material away and have the children experiment with their paints to discover a satisfying way to create water. If any of them decide to make ponds, remind them that perspective will make it quite narrow from the near to far shore. Encourage them to add other details for emphasis and interest, such as boats and people.

Mountains Take Many Forms

LEVEL 6

See
ACTIVITIES
39 *and* 67

SUGGESTED MATERIALS: Light blue or other drawing paper 12″ × 18″, crayons or chalk, and Plasticene.

If the children have never seen mountains, it might be worthwhile to have them model some in Plasticene before painting. Direct their observation to the various types of peaks and ridges, using many pictures. If there are mountains nearby, the pictures can be used to sharpen the children's perception of detail. When the children realize the basic form of mountains, they can experiment with ways to show this form on paper. Using the side of a crayon and applying pressure to one end of the line drawn accentuates surfaces that are curving away. Help the children to see the bluish purple haze over distant mountains. Yellow over the foothills will make them seem nearer.

Sketching Trees

LEVEL 7

See
ACTIVITY 64

SUGGESTED MATERIALS: White drawing paper 9″ × 12″ and soft primary pencils or their equivalent in drawing pencils.

Spend some time with the class looking at trees and reviewing concepts developed on previous levels. Direct their attention to shape and line differences, as well as the definition of large masses by dark and light. If sufficient time has been spent sharpening their perception, the students will complete their sketches with enthusiasm and confidence. Emphasize catching the shape of a particular tree and the feeling of its form.

Stormy Skies

LEVEL 7

See
ACTIVITY 59

SUGGESTED MATERIALS: Heavy white paper 16″ × 20″ or 12″ × 18″, big water-color brushes (perhaps No. 10), water colors, and sponges.

An imminent storm would be ideal for motivating this activity. Lacking this, collect pictures of stormy skies, preferably in water color. Direct student attention to the dramatic effect of strong diagonals in the sky. Suggest that they dampen their paper, then sponge off puddles. Have them mix a large quantity of dark bluish-black paint into which to dip their brush. After touching the tip in black paint, they can draw it across their paper to create strong effects. Something simple such as a few leafless trees might be silhouetted later against the sky.

Roads and Scenery

LEVEL 7

See
ACTIVITY 40

SUGGESTED MATERIALS: White 12″ × 18″ paper, newsprint 12″ × 18″, India ink, pens, water colors, and brushes.

Show the class the effect that the strong line direction of a road has on the design of a picture. Suggest that the students experiment on newsprint with sketches that include roads going in different directions. Remind them that roads become very narrow in the distance, usually diminishing to a line within a few miles. The boys will probably want to include cars in their final picture on white paper. The water color, in varied hues, can be flooded on before or after the sketches are detailed in India ink. Emphasize that this is not a coloring exercise and that colors should run into each other.

Country Scenes

LEVEL 7

See
ACTIVITIES
27 and 36

SUGGESTED MATERIALS: Drawing paper 12″ × 18″, newsprint 12″ × 18″, tempera paint, and easel brushes. The brushes should have firm bristles straight across the top.

Direct the attention of the class to the varied textures in a country scene by having them either observe one in actuality or view pictures. Guide them to perceive the line directions of the texture as well as the mixture of hues. Suggest that they experiment on newsprint with the textural effects made by the bristles of an almost dry brush. Have them plan a scene on the drawing paper with the principles of design in mind and then paint it, using dry-brush effects to create texture.

Scientific Drawing

LEVEL 8

See
ACTIVITY 65

SUGGESTED MATERIALS: White drawing paper 9″ × 12″, pen, and India ink.

Help the class understand that very little creativity is involved in accurate, detailed drawing, but that, since there is an occasional need for it in their studies, they should learn how to do it. Careful observation of the whole object, and then perception of the relationships of the parts to the whole, is the key to this type of drawing. Help the students to decide on the scale they should use, i.e., life-size, half-size, or double life-size. Suggest that they draw the entire object very lightly first, and then, after checking size relationships, go on to the details. After a final check for accuracy, the lines can be inked in.

Trees in Water Color

LEVEL 8

See
ACTIVITY 64

SUGGESTED MATERIALS: Heavy white paper 16″ × 20″ or 12″ × 18″, water colors, water pans, and large water-color brushes (No. 10, perhaps).

This activity builds directly on the observation and sketching of trees suggested for level 7. Use water-color paintings of outdoor scenes to suggest to the class that the medium usually requires exaggerated contrasts in value to bring out the form of foliage. Indicate also that water colors lose their freshness if changes are made once the brush has placed the color on the paper. The key to painting trees in water colors is careful perception of dark-to-light values, which are then painted simply, directly, and with some exaggeration. After experimentation, encourage the students to plan a simple outdoor scene featuring trees. Emphasize the fresh simplicity characteristic of the medium.

Clouds

LEVEL 8

See
ACTIVITY 66

SUGGESTED MATERIALS: Heavy white paper 16″ × 20″ or 12″ × 18″, big water-color brushes (perhaps No. 10), water-color paints, sponges, and rubber cement with brush applicators.

Choose a day when clouds are many and varied in the sky. Enjoy their changing shapes with the class. Indicate that rubber cement can be lightly spread to define the white space for a cloud in a water color. Help them to perceive that clouds become smaller nearer to the horizon. The sky color is painted on in a wash that goes over the dry rubber cement. Later the rubber cement is rubbed off with the fingers. This method can be used to reserve space for branches and other objects appearing against the sky. Encourage the students to plan a simple water-color scene emphasizing clouds.

Outdoor Scenes

LEVEL **8**

See
ACTIVITY 27

SUGGESTED MATERIALS: Heavy white paper 16″ × 20″ or 12″ × 18″, water-color paints, large water-color brushes (perhaps No. 10), water pans, cardboard 5″ × 8″, scissors, and rulers.

This is the first water-color painting for which it is recommended that the class remain outside to view the scene. Presumably the students have experienced all the dozen prior activities with water color on this and previous levels. Suggest that they make "finders" by cutting a 4″ × 6″ rectangle from a piece of 5″ × 8″ cardboard. The frame remaining is moved around the outdoor landscape to assist the students in locating an interesting area to paint. Remind them that their first object should be to create a good picture, and that if the design requires shifting or omitting objects, they should do it freely. Emphasize spontaneity and contrast.

SECTION SEVEN

Using Craft Experiences in Elementary–School Art

OBJECTIVES

To develop facility in the use of tools.

To create awareness of the uses and limitations of various materials by individual exploration.

To increase appreciation and respect for good craftsmanship without setting standards impossible for the child to achieve.

Crafts chosen for this section of the continuum are of the type that can be developed into a lifelong interest. The skills of the early levels are expanded with the older children so that they will feel the real satisfaction of the good craftsmen. The approach, however, is still experimental. No step-by-step directions are given. Leaders may find additional details in the first part of this book or in the craft books listed in the bibliography. For example, Babcock and Gerbracht's book, *Industrial Arts for Grades K-6*, is particularly recommended for teachers who feel hesitant about handling woodworking projects with children because of their own lack of experience with tools.

Ceramic Animals

LEVEL I

SUGGESTED MATERIALS: Lumps of Plasticene or water-base potter's clay about 3″ in diameter and a protected surface to work on.

For the children's first experiences with clay, encourage them to manipulate it and to get acquainted with it. One day, when the clay has become pliable from handling, suggest that it might be fun to slowly, and carefully, pull out legs for an animal from the big lump. Ask how many legs most animals have, then indicate that the neck and head can also be gradually pulled out. Make it seem quite dramatic and exciting to have created an animal. Praise the appearance of additional details. Save the products only if there is sufficient clay available for many more explorations.

Rubber-Ball Puppets

LEVEL I

SUGGESTED MATERIALS: Rubber balls with air inside (if possible, old tennis balls), colored paper scraps, yarn, scissors, paste, and pieces of cloth.

Have the children bring to school old rubber balls about the size of tennis balls. Use a sharp, small knife blade to cut a ¾″ hole for a finger in each ball. (Do not allow the children to do this; it is too dangerous.) Show the children how their puppets will work by poking an index finger, covered with a piece of material, into the hole in a ball. Wriggling the fingers creates the action. Give the children freedom to cut and paste features on their puppets. Small groups might improvise a play. The balls can be reused for other characters by soaking them to remove the paper.

Wooden Boats

LEVEL 1

See
ACTIVITY 76

SUGGESTED MATERIALS: Boards of varied lengths, wood scraps, claw hammers, C clamps, if possible a low sawhorse or a bench or other place to work, a pound of 4D common nails, enamel paints, each with a separate brush, and solvent to clean the brushes.

Take a few pieces of scrap wood and arrange them informally in different positions as the class discusses boats they can make for themselves. Explain that in order to fasten pieces of wood together securely they will have to learn to hammer carefully. Show them how the hammer should be held—comfortably in one hand, well away from its head. The other hand holds the nail while it is lightly tapped with the hammer two or three times. Then the fingers are removed and the nailing is completed. If a nail is crooked and can't be tapped straight, a piece of scrap wood can be pushed up against the nail as a rest for the head of the hammer while the claw removes the nail. Let the children create their boats freely and imaginatively. Protect the children's clothes with aprons and cover the table when the painting is going on. Clean the brushes in turpentine when it is finished.

Stitched Designs

LEVEL 1

SUGGESTED MATERIALS: About 1½ yards of material with an open mesh for a wall hanging, assorted yarn, big needles (those used for leather lacing are simplest to use), scraps of cloth, needles, thread, straight pins, and pin cushions.

Ask children to bring to class yarn of any length, even short pieces. Gather scraps of material and demonstrate how yarn can be woven in and out of mesh threads to make a gay design. Plan, with the children, for them to take turns creating designs within a top and bottom border, leaving the middle area clear for appliqué. Encourage the children to experiment with cutting shapes from pieces of material and pinning them to the cloth in the section reserved for the principal design. When the class likes the effect, show them how to sew, using a simple stitch. Pink the edges first, if possible. Have thread knotted on needles and available on a nearby pin cushion.

Pinch Bowls

LEVEL 2

SUGGESTED MATERIALS: Clay, preferably with a water base for firing, small tools such as nails for scratching designs, a protected surface to work on, and glaze if a kiln is available.

Give each child a ball of clay about 1½″ to 2″ in diameter. Encourage the class to manipulate the clay until it is pliable, then have them make it again into a ball. Tell them to push their thumbs into the center of the clay ball to gradually form a bowl. Next have them hold the bowl up and, with both thumbs inside, turn and shape it until the wall is about ¼″ thick. The next day ask them to take their bowls and decide whether they need any more poking or patting. If they want to make ash trays, this is the time to gouge out an indentation in the top for resting cigarettes. Suggest that nails, sticks, or fingernails be used to make a textural pattern on the outside of the bowl. Allow the bowl to dry at least a week. Glaze and fire it if there are facilities for doing so.

Simple Printing

LEVEL 2

SUGGESTED MATERIALS: Potatoes or carrots, dull paring knives or vegetable peelers, Plasticene, big nails or tongue blades, old newspaper, powdered tempera paint, and absorbent paper 12″ × 18″, such as news-print.

See
Activity 72
Have the children bring in vegetables or else use Plasticene that has become discolored and dry. Discuss gift wrappings, or printed cloth as having a design that has been stamped over and over to cover the surface. Tell them that if they make a design by cutting lines in the vegetables or the Plasticene they can use it to print all over their papers. A pad for printing can be made by dampening many layers of newspaper and sprinkling the top layer with powdered tempera and a little water. They can press the vegetable design into the paint, and then on the newsprint. Extra newspaper under the newsprint makes a more resilient surface.

Wooden Airplanes

LEVEL 2

See
Activity 76

SUGGESTED MATERIALS: Boards of various lengths and wood scraps, a crosscut saw, C clamps, a low sawhorse or a bench or other place to fasten the C clamp and wood for sawing, a claw hammer, 4D common nails, assorted tempera paints, and a pressure spray can of lacquer.

Discuss airplanes with the class and then tell them they can make their own from available wood. Show them how to saw so that they can achieve results that satisfy them. The best tool for young children is the crosscut panel saw. The board to be cut may be clamped to the bench with an additional piece of wood held by the C clamp as a cutting guide. Holding the saw at approximately a 45° angle to the board, pull back several times to establish a groove. Short back-and-forth strokes should be soon followed by long, slow cuts. Near the end, short strokes are better again. Both hands on the saw will prove safer and give better guidance. Review the nailing procedures learned in level 1. Allow the children to improvise freely and later to paint their airplanes. Spray the airplanes with lacquer for water protection.

Simple Appliqués

LEVEL 2

SUGGESTED MATERIALS: Cotton yardage, scraps of cloth, heavy thread, straight pins, darning needles, and scissors.

Discuss with the class their need for a gay cloth hanging, either decorative, or to serve as drapes. If there are favorite stories that can be used as themes, plan small groups to work on each one. Presumably the children have had much experience using cut paper to make pictures. Explain that cutting cloth into shapes and pinning it onto the background is similar to cutting paper and pasting it, only with cloth they have the fun of stitching it later. Have each group evaluate the work after all the pieces are pinned on, to decide whether they want to change any details. Pink the edges or pin them under before the children take turns sewing as near the edge as possible. Upper-grade girls might be borrowed to help thread needles and supervise. Don't expect even stitches. The result will be childlike and wonderful.

Simple Dishes

LEVEL 3

See
Activity 74

SUGGESTED MATERIALS: Water-base clay, flat plywood or Masonite boards 12″ × 18″, strips of wood ¼″ × 18″ (have several boards prepared by older boys if enough wood is available), rolling pins, and pieces of old cotton sheeting or cheesecloth.

Have the children work in small groups, each group to make a clay form that resembles an upside-down bowl or dish. See that they press in the sides so that it does not slope out too far. They will enjoy patting and poking it until the surface is even. Cover it with a single layer of dampened cloth. Set out a board with two strips of ¼″ × 18″ wood nailed parallel, about 9″ or 10″ apart (no wider than the length of roller or rolling pin). Show the children how placing the rolling pin so the ends stay on the strips enables them to roll even ¼″ thick sheets of clay to place over their molds. See Activity 74 in Part One for further detailed directions.

Wooden Birdhouses

LEVEL 3

See
ACTIVITY 76

SUGGESTED MATERIALS: Boards of uniform width, possibly 1″ × 8″ fir without knotholes if available, a hand drill, a coping saw, a crosscut saw, C clamps or a vise, a low sawhorse or bench or other place to work if possible, a pound of 4D common nails, enamel paint, brushes, and solvent to clean the brushes.

With pieces of wood in hand, discuss with the children the simplest methods of creating a birdhouse. The house should be a sturdy shelter from wind and rain with a small access hole. It might be tent-shaped, made from three pieces of board with triangular pieces to fit the front and back. The problem of fastening the base to the roof can be solved by nails that are anchored by being driven downward, at an angle, from the side roof into the base. Have the children work out possibilities with cardboard first. Demonstrate the use of a hand drill by placing the end of the twist drill bit in the center of the circle drawn on the wood to provide entrance for the bird. With a slight pressure turn the crank handle clockwise through the wood. Continue to turn it in the same direction while withdrawing drill. Release one end of the coping-saw blade, insert the blade in the hole, refasten it, and proceed to saw the outline of the hole. Review the nailing, sawing, and painting procedures learned on earlier levels. Don't expect perfection in craftsmanship at this level!

Inner-Tube Printing

LEVEL 3

See
ACTIVITY 72

SUGGESTED MATERIALS: Old inner tubes cut into small 4″ × 6″ pieces, scraps of flat wood such as plywood also 4″ × 6″, pointed scissors, white glue, absorbent paper about 5″ × 8″, and either water-soluble printer's ink with brayers or powdered tempera paint with damp newspaper pads.

Discuss the large variety of holiday symbols that are simple enough to be cut out of the inner tubing. Encourage the children to repeat some symbols several times or to vary their size to produce variety. Show them how they can glue the rubber onto the wood. Praise ingenuity in filling the area with interesting designs. When the glue is dry, the ink can be rolled over the surface of the rubber with a brayer or the design can be pressed into damp powdered tempera. Then the design can be printed on absorbent paper. Let the children write their greetings on the back or inner page of the card. Words are too difficult to cut out on this level.

Stick Puppets

LEVEL 3

SUGGESTED MATERIALS: Strips of wood about ¼″ × ¼″ × 18″, construction paper or thin cardboard, scissors, paste, and paper-fasteners.

142

Discuss with the class the favorite stories they might dramatize with stick puppets. Have them establish an average size for adult and child characters, probably about 10″ and 6″. Tell them that stick puppets are made from colored construction paper cut and pasted together. They are then attached securely to a stick so that the stick supports the full length of the body and ends just short of the top of the head. Extra action can be added by joining arms to the bodies with paper fasteners and then stapling the hands to an extra stick. Drape a blanket over the backs of a row of chairs and have the children sit behind the chairs on the floor to operate the puppets. With a little practice they will be able to keep their puppets up and moving and their hands down out of sight.

Puzzles

LEVEL 4

SUGGESTED MATERIALS: Flat thin pieces of wood, probably ¼″ plywood, assorted enamel paints, brushes, and turpentine or assorted tempera paints and shellac with brushes, coping saws (preferably with screw-type handles), and C clamps.

Help the children to plan simple but interesting pictures to fit their pieces of wood. Emphasize that the paints used to paint the picture should cover the top of the wood completely. Have the children brush on shellac if tempera paints are used. When the surface is dry, they can mark uneven divisions on the underside. After clamping the wood to the table with a C clamp, they use a coping saw, keeping the blade vertical to the surface of the wood, to saw on the lines. Teach the children to change blades; it is simply a matter of turning the screw-type handle and checking the direction on the teeth of the blade point. When work is cut in an upright position, the teeth should point away from the handle. When work is flat, the teeth point toward the handle. Let the class decide whether they want to give the finished puzzles to a lower grade, or to charity.

Slabware Dishes

LEVEL 4

See
ACTIVITY 74

SUGGESTED MATERIALS: Boards with ¼″ guide strips for rolling out clay (see level 3, Simple Dishes), water-base clay, rolling pins, rulers 18″ long, heavy paper 6″ × 9″, and glaze if a kiln is available.

Explain to the class that a free-form shape is curved, but is not evenly round as a circle is. Have them design free-form shapes, with perhaps a simple indentation, on heavy paper. After rolling out a ¼″ sheet of clay they place their paper shape on top of it and cut it out of the clay with a dull knife. This is the base of the dish. Next they place a ruler on the clay sheet and cut a rectangular strip of clay the length and width of the ruler. One edge of this strip must be firmly fastened around the edge of the free form as the side wall. Marking light X's along the ¼″ on the edge of the base and using thin clay "slip" as glue will help. The two ends of the strip must also be fastened in this way. Glaze and fire the dish when dry.

Pebble Mosaics

LEVEL 4

See
ACTIVITY 71

SUGGESTED MATERIALS: Assorted flat stones, a strong cardboard lid reinforced with paper strips at the corners, plaster of Paris or commercial grout mixture, molasses, and shellac or lacquer.

Have the children collect beautiful, rather flat stones. Encourage them to place them in three boxes according to their value—dark, medium, or light. The first arrangement of the pebbles into a design, within the lid of a sturdy cardboard box, might be a group project.

Emphasize the need for value contrast between the areas for a good design. A thin molasses mixture will act as glue to keep the stones in place. Pour plaster of Paris (see the directions on level 6 in this section) or commercial grout mixture to fill the lid. Let it set. Tear away the cardboard and reverse the mosaic. The stones can be shellacked or sprayed with lacquer to make them shiny.

Cross-Stitch Samplers

LEVEL 4

SUGGESTED MATERIALS: Paper 9″ × 12″ divided into ¼″ squares, plain cotton cloth pieces about 9″ × 12″, odds and ends of yarn, embroidery thread, needles with large eyes, and scissors.

Display samplers from early days, or substitute pictures. Explain to the class that many were made by children their ages. Have them design their simple samplers by marking *X*'s within the squares of their papers. Help them to staple their papers to cotton cloth the same size. Using available yarn and embroidery thread, the children do cross-stitches through the paper and cloth following their designs. When they have finished, they remove the paper completely and possibly fringe the edges. Covers for the dolls' beds in the kindergarten could be made by sewing the pieces together.

Bowls Made with Coils

LEVEL 5

SUGGESTED MATERIALS: Water-base or potter's clay, dull knives and flat sticks such as tongue blades, a protected surface to work on, and glaze if a kiln is available.

Explain to the children that many beautiful Indian bowls were made by building rows of coils, one on top of the other. After wedging the clay, have the children practice rolling coils evenly, trying to get them about ½″ thick. The base can be made by patting a ball of clay to a uniform thickness and then cutting an even circle around a jar top or other guide. Demonstrate how to lay the first row of coils around the edge of the base. Use soft clay "slip" as glue. Emphasize joining the two ends of the coils carefully, using slip and firm pressure, before going on to the row above. The bowl can be built up to almost any desired height, but all the joining must be done firmly with slip. Explain that careless work cannot be saved because it would crack apart in time. Some highly coordinated children may want to eliminate the appearance of coils entirely. This should not be a class goal, however. After the bowls have dried a day, have the children check them for even height. The lowest point along the top edge can be measured and the remainder cut to that height with a knife. After a week the bowls can be fired, glazed, and then refired if facilities are available.

"House" Book Racks

LEVEL 5

See
ACTIVITY 76

SUGGESTED MATERIALS: Wood, preferably clear fir, about 1″ × 8″ × 2′ for each child, Manila paper 6″ × 9″, C clamps, coping saws, tempera paint, brushes, medium- and fine-grade sandpaper, a claw hammer, 1″ finishing nails, lacquer in a pressure can or shellac, brushes, and solvent.

Discuss the distinctive features of houses such as variations in the number of windows and the placement of doors. Suggest that the children draw their homes, or houses they would like to live in, on paper, making them about 6″ high by the width of the available board. When finished, the drawing is cut out and traced twice on two pieces of wood. Have the children use clamps to hold the wood while they are cutting it with the coping saw. Sanding lightly but thoroughly with the grain will make the surface smooth. Let the tempera paint used to paint the houses dry thoroughly before spraying it with lacquer, or brushing it lightly with shellac. The two houses are nailed to opposite ends of the remaining piece of wood (about 12″ in length). The books are placed on this board, leaning on the houses for support.

Individual Seed Mosaics

LEVEL 5

Part One,
ACTIVITY 71

SUGGESTED MATERIALS: Heavy cardboard or flat scraps of wood about 6″ × 8″, assorted dried beans, possibly alcohol and food coloring, white glue or rubber cement, lacquer in a pressure can or shellac, brushes, and solvent.

Purchase small quantities of dried beans of various hues. They can be colored by being dipped in alcohol tinted with food coloring if more variety is needed. (Alcohol is poisonous and should be kept away from the children.) Give the children pieces of heavy cardboard or flat scraps of wood on which to plan a design with a simple but interesting shape for emphasis. Emphasize the need for a strong contrast of color or value in a mosaic. The beans should be glued as close together as possible. Spraying the finished surface with lacquer or brushing it with shellac protects it.

String Puppets

LEVEL 5

See
ACTIVITY 70

SUGGESTED MATERIALS: Cotton sheeting, Manila paper 9″ × 12″, needles, thread, assorted cloth pieces, stuffing material, yarn, crayon, black button cord, wax, scissors, and 6″ sticks.

Show the class a puppet made with the directions given for Activity 70 in Part One. As the children examine it and try making it walk, discuss story possibilities for a set of characters they can make. Have them bring in old clean sheets and pieces of cloth as well as clean cotton and nylon for stuffing. Pieces of yarn are useful too. When all is ready, proceed as explained in Activity 70. Clothes for the puppets can be made by interested girls, or dolls' clothes brought in. Waxing the strings will prevent excessive tangling. The stage can be improvised from a large packing box obtained from a local store, and scenery can be painted to fit the back wall of the stage. Dolls' furniture will do for most props. Most classes like to divide into committees for this project.

Clay Pitchers

LEVEL 6

SUGGESTED MATERIALS: Water-base potter's clay, tools for scratching (large nails will do), tongue blades, a protected surface to work on, and glaze, if a kiln is available.

Review with the class the procedure for making a bowl with coils (see level 5). Have them draw the simple shape of the pitcher they wish to make on light cardboard and cut it out. Either side of the background left after the shape is cut out can be used as a template to hold against the clay form as it is built up. This ensures that the finished pitcher will resemble the sketch. Show children how the spout can be gently pressed into the top edge before the pitcher is put away to dry. The next day, they can roll a coil of clay for the handle. The pitcher is marked with X's scratched into the surface at the two places the handle will be fastened. Slip is used as glue, and the handle firmly welded to the pitcher. Dry, fire, glaze, and refire it as facilities permit.

Wooden Trays

LEVEL 6

See
ACTIVITY 76

SUGGESTED MATERIALS: Rectangular pieces of ¼″ plywood, perhaps 12″ × 18″, odd-sized wood scraps, fine-grade sandpaper, 4D nails and tacks, metal stripping ½″ wide, wax crayons, black tempera paint, black semigloss enamel, brushes, lacquer in a pressure can or shellac, and solvent to clean the brushes.

Have the children wrap fine sandpaper around blocks of wood and lightly sand the surface of their rectangular pieces of plywood. While they are working, discuss with them designs that they can use to decorate the center of their trays. Encourage them to draw the designs directly on the wood. Imaginary flowers are often used. Challenge them to think of other ideas, too. Mistakes can be erased with sandpaper. The design can be colored with bright hues of wax crayon put on heavily. Have them paint the completed design with black tempera paint. When dry, the tray can be sprayed with lacquer or brushed with shellac. Blocks of scrap wood are sanded and nailed to either end of the tray for handles. Strips of thin metal edging can be tacked along the outside edge. This, and the handle, might be painted with black semigloss enamel.

Plaster-of-Paris Plaques

LEVEL 6

SUGGESTED MATERIALS: Plaster of Paris, a large pan, and miscellaneous carving tools such as old chisels, gauges, screw drivers, and paring knives.

Collect some bas-relief that is raised slightly above the background, or pictures of it. There are many examples in books on sculpture. Discuss the works with the class. Ask them to bring in cardboard boxes or box lids, so they can carve in low-relief. When ready, fill a large pan three-fourths full of water. Drop handfuls of plaster evenly over the surface of the water. Continue this until the plaster no longer sinks, but rests in little inch-high islands on the surface. *Only then* dip in and mix it well with the hands. No more plaster can be added. Pour it immediately into containers. Allow it to harden an hour or two. Tear away the cardboard. Children will find they can carve easily with knives and other tools. Jungle or other animal scenes make interesting carvings. N.B.: Wipe the excess plaster from the large pan immediately and place it in a trash can. *Don't* let plaster get into the sink drains.

Metal Modeling

LEVEL 6

SUGGESTED MATERIALS: 34-gauge copper or brass foil, an assortment of wooden tools, sticks, steel wool in a holder, lacquer, brushes, solvent, and if needed escutcheon nails and a tack hammer.

Explain that the metal foil is soft enough to be modeled by pressure from either side with a wooden stick. Whole areas can be pressed out by rubbing them with the end of a tongue blade if the metal foil is resting on a resilient surface, such as several inches thick of old newspaper. Thin lines or texture can also be created with other tools. Emphasize the need for a simple, dominant, yet interesting form for the center of interest in the design, and variety in line and texture in the background. Give the children steel wool in a holder for polishing the finished piece, then spray or brush on lacquer. They can tack the metal foil on wood with escutcheon nails, or mount and frame it for a picture.

Linoleum Prints

LEVEL 7

See
ACTIVITY 72

SUGGESTED MATERIALS: Linoleum (battleship linoleum in brown 12″ × 12″ pieces is the least expensive), linoleum gouges or sharp knives, brayers, water-base printer's ink, and absorbent paper such as newsprint or Manila paper.

Examine, with the class, many good woodcuts. Direct their attention to the dark-and-light pattern, and the areas of texture. The success of their designs depends on clear contrast and the use of texture to emphasize the important idea. If greeting cards are the objective, stress a "different idea." All letters must be cut out to read backwards so they will print correctly. The linoleum needs to be cut at least ⅛ inch deep to prevent the lines from filling with ink. The ink can be squeezed out on an easily cleaned surface such as glass. The brayer rolls the ink onto the linoleum design. If the first print needs improving, students can wash the linoleum, dry it thoroughly, and make additional cuts. After changes, a new print can be made.

Covered Bowls

LEVEL 7

SUGGESTED MATERIALS: Water-base potter's clay, modeling tools, tongue blades, a protected surface to work on, and glaze if a kiln is available.

This project presumes that the students have done the ceramic projects on the previous two levels. Have them build a bowl carefully by the coil method, continuing until the top is almost closed. A slight circular opening will remain after the last row of coils. If it is necessary to work over a period of days, the top coil should be kept moist with a damp rag. After the top has been reached, allow the piece to dry for a day. Have the students carefully mark off where the cover should be, and cut it on that line with a sharp knife. Caution them to handle the lid carefully while filling in the hole with clay and then forming a handle for lifting purposes. Dry the bowl thoroughly, fire it, glaze it, and refire it as facilities allow.

Stenciling on Textiles

LEVEL 7

See
ACTIVITY 68

SUGGESTED MATERIALS: Stencil paper or heavy waxed sheets from mimeograph stencils, sharp knives or single-edged razor blades in holders, washed and ironed cloth, textile paint, and short, stiff-bristled brushes.

Discuss possible projects such as curtains, place mats, skirts, or a decorative wall hanging. Show the students peasant designs, perhaps in some of the wonderful, imaginative illustrations in books for young children. Put these away and have the children evolve their own designs. Show them that in cutting they will have the problem of leaving some areas completely detached, unless small bridges are made to the rest of the design. When the cutting is completed, the stencil is fastened or held firmly on the cloth while the brush with *very little paint on it* is daubed on the open spaces. To create solid areas repeated daubing is better than too much paint at once. Follow the directions on the paint jar for setting the colors.

Jewelry in a Press Mold

LEVEL 7

SUGGESTED MATERIALS: Plaster of Paris, small boxes, knives, and potter's clay.

Review the procedure described in level 6 for making plaster of Paris. Have students bring small boxes and fill them with plaster. Examine photographs, or bring in well-designed jewelry. Explain that a pair of earrings or a multipiece necklace can be made by carving a single piece in reverse in the plaster as a mold, then pressing clay into it. The carved shape should be distinctive because very little added design is feasible. Have them press clay firmly into the finished carving. After 15 to 20 minutes they can pry it gently loose, or prop it so it will fall out in an hour or so. Evaluate it and have them recarve portions if necessary. Students can make as many copies as they wish, although the moisture absorbency of the plaster may be reduced if the plaster is used without pauses for drying it out. Allow the copies to dry, fire them, glaze them, and refire them as facilities permit.

Weaving

LEVEL 8

SUGGESTED MATERIALS depend on the loom and type of weaving chosen by the student.

See ACTIVITY 73

Plan, if possible, a visit to a local weaver's studio to help the class realize what weaving involves. Committees might be appointed to investigate and report on various types of looms, including Navajo, backstrap, tapestry, and foot-power looms. Some students may wish to experiment and build looms of varying complexity. Others may prefer the simple cardboard loom explained in Activity 73, Part One.

Carved Sculpture

LEVEL 8

SUGGESTED MATERIALS: Vermiculite and cement (available at low cost from a builders' supply company), a metal bucket, cardboard cartons, old screw drivers, chisels, white soap, and paring knives for finer work.

Bring in any available sculpture or photographs of good, simple work in three dimensions. Some students, who like to work on a small scale, may choose to carve in soap, using a small knife. Others may bring in shoe boxes or grocery cartons, and plan to work on a larger scale. The vermiculite and cement are mixed dry in either a 4-to-1 or a 3-to-1 proportion. Place the mixture in the bucket and add water while stirring until the mixture is thoroughly moist but not liquid. Pour it into cardboard containers and allow it to set overnight. Then remove it from the cartons by tearing the cardboard. For the first few weeks students can use paring knives or anything else that will cut or scrape. The material eventually gets quite hard. Caution them to keep paper underneath their work to collect the scraps. Emphasize the need to turn the carvings every few minutes to develop all sides of them as part of the design.

Ceramic Tile Mosaics

LEVEL 8

SUGGESTED MATERIALS: Tile (source noted below), clay and glaze if needed, plywood or Masonite pieces, a hammer, strong white glue, a grout mixture, sponges, a rolling pin, and knives.

Visit an example of mosaic art or show the class many pictures of good mosaics. If there is a cooperative local tile-setter, he will quite likely be glad to give the students boxes of scrap pieces that are of no use to him. Lacking this resource, have the students roll out clay with a rolling pin to an even ¼″ thickness. Allow it to become stiff or leather-hard overnight. Then brush on varied one-fire glazes. Score the clay sheets into small pieces about ½″ square. (The knife should not go quite through the clay.) Dry it thoroughly, then fire it. Ceramic tile from a tile-setter will have to be broken with a hammer into usable small pieces. Have the students plan their mosaic so that its center of interest will contrast strongly with its background. Have them glue the tile to plywood or Masonite with strong white glue, and then mix grout and water to a thick cream and cover the tile with it. The cream is shaken and tapped into cracks. Immediately afterward the surface is wiped with a barely damp sponge until the tiles are clean.

Simple Silk-Screen Printing

LEVEL **8**

See
ACTIVITY 75

SUGGESTED MATERIALS: Cardboard boxes, cotton organdy that has been washed and ironed, gummed brown paper tape, waxed paper, knives, a stapler, shellac, brushes, solvent, finger paint, squeegees or smooth wooden sticks, Manila or similar absorbent paper, and old newspapers.

Explain to the students that this widely used process is an elaboration of the simple stencil. The cloth used acts to hold the parts of the stencil together. The design for the first experience ought to be kept simple. Have the class bring in firm, shallow cardboard boxes, or box lids. After they cut an opening the size of their design in the lid, cotton organdy should be stapled on the inside. The piece must be large enough to overlap the cardboard by at least an inch. All exposed parts of the cardboard box are taped with brown paper, including the overlap, and then brushed with shellac. The wax paper from which the design is cut should be the size of the bottom of the box, although the design itself must be smaller than the opening. For printing, have the working surface covered with newspaper, and have first the Manila paper and then the wax-paper design placed conveniently with the organdy portion of the screen on top of them. Finger paint is placed inside, at one end of the box. It is dragged across the organdy with the squeegee to make the print underneath. When the box is lifted, the Manila paper may have to be peeled off. The wax paper remains on the organdy until the number of copies needed have been printed. More than one color can be achieved with additional stencils.

Grade 1

Grade 2

Grade
3

Grade
4

Examples of
Children's Art

Grade
5

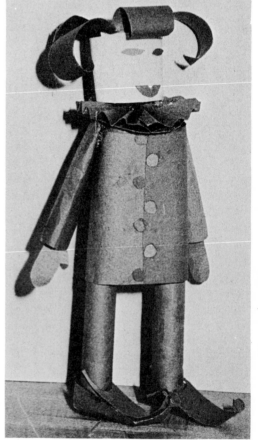

Grade
6

150

This evaluation form has been used for several years by student- and in-service-teachers who have tried the various continuum activities with children. The experimental nature of the continuum requires this continuous evaluation. The author would appreciate receiving any information of this type, or other suggestions, from users of this book. Please send material through the publishers.

REPORT FORM FOR ART ACTIVITIES FROM CONTINUUM

Continuum Unit _____

Title of Activity _____

Grade Level of Class Doing Project _____

Time Required for Average Student to Complete Project _____

Difficulties Encountered by Teacher _____

_____

_____

_____

Difficulties Encountered by Students _____

_____

_____

_____

Do you consider the activity a satisfactory one for students of this grade? _____

_____

Comments _____

_____

_____

BIBLIOGRAPHY

Part I: Additional Resources

ANDERSON, DONALD M. *Elements of Design.* New York: Holt, Rinehart and Winston, Inc., 1961.

ARGIRO, LARRY. *Mosaic Art Today.* Scranton, Pa.: International Textbook Co., 1961.

ART DIRECTORS' CLUB OF NEW YORK. *Art Directing for Visual Communication.* New York: Hastings House, 1957.

BABCOCK, ROBERT, AND CARL GERBRACHT. *Industrial Arts for Grades K-6.* Milwaukee: The Bruce Publishing Co., 1959.

BALL, VICTORIA KLOSS. *The Art of Interior Design.* New York: The Macmillan Co., 1961.

BATCHELDER, MARJORIE, AND V. L. COMER. *Puppets and Plays: A Creative Approach.* New York: Harper & Brothers, 1956.

BATES, KENNETH F. *Basic Design.* Cleveland: The World Publishing Company, 1960.

BECKER, EDITH C. *Adventures with Scissors and Paper.* Scranton, Pa.: International Textbook Co., 1959.

BENZ, M. *Flowers Free Form: Interpretive Design.* Houston, Texas: San Jacinto Publishing Co., 1960.

BLACK, ARTHUR. *How to Draw the Human Figure.* New York: McGraw-Hill Book Co., Inc., 1950.

BRION, MARCEL, ET AL. *Art since 1945.* New York: Harry N. Abrams, Inc., 1958.

BROOKS, LEONARD. *Watercolor: A Challenge.* New York: Reinhold Publishing Corp., 1957.
——————. *Course in Wash Drawing.* New York: Reinhold Publishing Corp., 1961.

BROWN, HARRIETTE J. *Handweaving: For Pleasure and Profit.* New York: Harper and Brothers, 1952.

CYPHERS, EMMA H. *Foliage Arrangement.* New York: Hearthside Press, 1956.

DORIVAL, BERNARD. *Twentieth Century French Painters,* 2 vols. New York: Universe Books, Inc., 1958.

ELGAR, FRANK. *Picasso.* New York: Frederick A. Praegar, Inc., 1957.

FAULKNER, RAY, EDWIN ZIEGFIELD, AND GEROLD HILL. *Art Today: An Introduction to the Fine and Functional Arts.* New York: Henry Holt & Co., Inc., 1956.

GAITSKELL, CHARLES D. *Children and Their Art.* New York: Harcourt, Brace & World, Inc., 1958.

GANNON, RUTH. *Winter Bouquets with Color.* New York: Thomas Y. Crowell Company, 1951.

GILLES, MARY DAVIS, *All about Modern Decorating.* New York: Harper & Brothers, 1948.

GROSS, FRED. *How to Work with Tools and Wood.* New York: Pocket Books, Inc., 1955.

HALD, ARTHUR, AND SVEN ERIK SKAWONIUS. *Contemporary Swedish Design.* New York: Pellegrini & Cudahy, 1951.

HAMMETT, CATHERINE. *Creative Crafts for Campers.* New York: Association Press, 1957.

HOAR, FRANK. *Pen and Ink Drawing.* New York: Studio Publications, Inc., 1955.

HOLME, K., AND K. FROST, EDITORS. *Decorative Art,* Volume 48. London: The Studio, Ltd., 1958.

JOHNSON, PAULINE. *Creating with Paper.* Seattle: University of Washington Press, 1958.

KAMINSKI, EDWARD B. *How to Draw.* New York: McGraw-Hill Book Co., Inc., 1949.

KEPES, GYÖRGY. *The New Landscape in Art and Science.* Chicago: Theobald & Co., 1956.

KUH, KATHERINE. *Art Has Many Faces.* New York: Harper & Brothers, 1951.

LAWSON, PHILIP J. *Practical Perspective Drawing.* New York: McGraw-Hill Book Co., Inc., 1943.

LEITH-ROSS, HARRY. *The Landscape Painter's Manual.* New York: Watson-Guptill Publications, Inc., 1956.

LEWIS, ROGER. *Weaving.* New York: Alfred A. Knopf, Inc., 1953.

LYNCH, JOHN. *Mobile Design.* New York: Studio Publications Inc., 1955.

McFEE, JUNE K. *Preparation for Art.* Belmont, Cal.: Wadsworth Publishing Co., Inc., 1961.

MATTIL, EDWARD L. *Meaning in Crafts*. Englewood Cliffs, N.J.: Prentice Hall, Inc., 1959.

Moderns and Their World. London: Phoenix House, Ltd., 1959.

MUSEUM OF MODERN ART. *Modern Drawings*. New York: Simon and Schuster, Inc., 1947.

NICOLAIDES, KIMON. *The Natural Way to Draw*. Boston: Houghton Mifflin Co., 1941.

NOMA, SEIROKU. *The Art of Clay*. Tokyo: Bijutsu Shuppan-sha, 1954.

NORTON, F. H. *Ceramics: An Illustrated Primer*. Garden City, N.Y.: Hanover House, 1960.

O'HARA, ELIOT. *Making the Brush Behave*. New York: Minton, Balch & Co., 1935.

PETERDI, GABOR. *Printmaking: Methods Old and New*. New York: The Macmillan Co., 1959.

POUSETTE-DART, NATHANIEL, EDITOR. *Art Directing*. Art Directors Club of New York. New York: Hastings House, 1957.

QUINN, VERNON. *Picture Map Geography of Asia*, rev. ed. Philadelphia: J. B. Lippincott Co., 1955.

RAND, PAUL. *Thoughts on Design*. New York: Wittenborn, Schultz, Inc., 1951.

RATHBUN, MARY C., AND BARTLETT H. HAYES, JR. *Layman's Guide to Modern Art*. New York: Oxford University Press, Inc., 1949.

RILEY, OLIVE. *Masks and Magic*. New York: Studio Publications, Inc., 1955.

ROGER-MARX, CLAUDE. *Raoul Dufy*. Paris: Fernand Hazen, 1950.

ROOD, JOHN. *Sculpture in Wood*. Minneapolis: University of Minnesota Press, 1950.

SAN LAZZARO, G. DI. *Klee*. London: Thames and Hudson, 1957.

SKEAPING, JOHN R. *Animal Drawing*. New York: Studio Publications, Inc., 1959.

SWEENEY, JAMES JOHNSON. *Henry Moore*. New York: Simon and Schuster, Inc., 1946.

WATSON, JANE WERNER. *The Golden History of the World*. New York: Simon and Schuster, Inc., 1955.

WERNER, ELSA JANE. *The Golden Geography*. New York: Simon and Schuster, Inc., 1952.

WIGHT, FREDERICK, ET AL. *Morris Graves*. Berkeley: University of California Press, 1956.

ZAIDENBERG, ARTHUR. *Out of Line*. New York: Crown Publishers, Inc., 1952.

ZWEIFEL, FRANCES W. *A Handbook of Biological Illustration*. Chicago: University of Chicago Press, 1961.

Part II: Books for Children to Enjoy

SYMBOLS: *L*, grades 1–3; *M*, grades 4–6; *U*, grades 7–8.

DESIGN AS THE MAIN EMPHASIS

L   BORTEN, HELEN. *Do You See What I See?* New York: Abelard-Schuman, Limited, 1959.

L-M-U   DOWNER, MARION. *Discovering Design*. New York: Lothrop Lee & Shepard Co., 1947.

M-U   HUGHES, LANGSTON. *The First Book of Rhythms*. New York: Franklin Watts, Inc., 1954.

L   KESSLER, LEONARD P. *What's in a Line?* New York: William R. Scott, Inc., 1951.

L-M   KIRN, ANN. *Full of Wonder*. Cleveland: The World Publishing Co., 1959.

L-M   MACAGY, DOUGLAS AND ELIZABETH. *Going for a Walk with a Line*. Garden City, New York: Doubleday & Co., 1959.

M-U   PASCHEL, HERBERT P. *The First Book of Color*. New York: Franklin Watts, Inc., 1959.

AN APPRECIATION OF ART AS THE MAIN EMPHASIS

M-U   CHASE, ALICE E. *Famous Paintings*. New York: The Platt & Munk Co., Inc., 1951.

M-U   HOLME, BRYAN. *Pictures to Live With*. New York: The Viking Press, Inc., 1959.

U   HILLYER, V. M., AND E. G. HUEY. *A Child's History of Art*. New York: Appleton-Century-Crofts, Inc., 1951.

M   KESSLER, LEONARD. *Art Is Everywhere*. New York: Dodd, Mead & Co., 1958.

M-U MANLEY, SEON. *Adventures in Making: Romance of Crafts Around the World.* New York: Vanguard Press, 1959.

M-U MUNRO, ELEANOR C. *The Golden Encyclopedia of Art.* New York: Golden Press, Inc., 1961.

L-M WEISGARD, LEONARD. *Treasures to See.* New York: Harcourt, Brace & World, Inc., 1956.

CRAFTS AS MAIN EMPHASIS

M-U HUNT, KARI, AND BERNICE CARLSON. *Masks and Mask-Makers.* New York: Abingdon Press, 1961.

L-M-U OTA, KOSHI, ET AL. *Printing for Fun.* New York: McDowell, Obolensky, Inc., 1958.

M-U TURNER, G. ALAN. *Creative Crafts for Everyone.* New York: Studio Publications, Inc., 1959.

L-M-U WEISS, HARVEY. *Clay, Wood, and Wire.* New York: William R. Scott, Inc., 1956.

M-U ————. *Paper, Ink, and Roller.* New York: William R. Scott, Inc., 1958.

U ZARCHY, HARRY. *Jewelry-Making and Enameling.* New York: Alfred A. Knopf, Inc., 1959.

U ————. *Let's Make a Lot of Things.* New York: Alfred A. Knopf, Inc., 1948.

List of Films Referred To in Book

The Adventures of the Asterisk, Guggenheim Museum, Distrib. Edward Harrison, 10 min., 1957.

Brush Techniques, Ency. Brit. Films, 11 min., 1947.

Discovering Color, Film Assoc. of Calif., 16 min., 1960.

Discovering Perspective, Film Assoc. of Calif., 14 min., 1962.

Discovering Texture, Film Assoc. of Calif., 17 min., 1961.

Line, Portafilms, 11 min., 1957.

Line and Art, Thorne Films, 11 min., 1960.

Making a Mobile, Bailey Films, 10 min., 1948.

Making of a Mural, Ency. Brit. Films, 10 min., 1947.

Mark Tobey: Artist, Orbit Films, Distrib. Brandon, 20 min., 1951.

Mosaic Experiments, Visual Ed. Films, Distrib. International Film Bureau, 20 min., 1958.

New Ways of Seeing, Contemporary Films, 15 min., 1954.

Painting Clouds, Ency. Brit. Films, 18 min., 1955.

Painting Crowds of People, Ency. Brit. Films, 11 min., 1956.

Painting Pictures about People, Inter. Film Bureau, 13 min., 1958.

Painting Reflections in Water, Ency. Brit. Films, 11 min., 1947.

Paper in the Round, Young America Films, Inc., 11 min., 1956.

Painting Trees with Eliot O'Hara, Ency. Brit. Films, 16 min., 1954.

The Purple Turtle, Association Films, 13½ min., 1961.

Answers to color test on page 17

MAROON	red	low	low
BROWN	orange	medium	low
PINK	red	high	low